T0270655

THE LEADERSHIP PIPELINE

THIRD
EDITION

THE
LEADERSHIP
PIPELINE

DEVELOPING
LEADERS IN THE
DIGITAL AGE

RAM CHARAN | STEPHEN DROTTER | JIM NOEL
KENT JONASEN

WILEY

Published by John Wiley & Sons, Inc., Hoboken, New Jersey.
Published simultaneously in Canada.

For general information on our other products and services or for technical support, please contact our Customer Care Department within the United States at (800) 762-2974, outside the United States at (317) 572-3993 or fax (317) 572-4002.

Wiley also publishes its books in a variety of electronic formats. Some content that appears in print may not be available in electronic formats. For more information about Wiley products, visit our web site at www.wiley.com.

Library of Congress Cataloging-in-Publication Data

Names: Charan, Ram, author.
Title: The leadership pipeline : leading in the digital age / Ram Charan, Stephen Drotter, Jim Noel, Kent Jonasen.
Description: Hoboken, New Jersey : John Wiley & Sons, Inc., [2024] | Earlier edition published in 2011.
Identifiers: LCCN 2023046444 (print) | LCCN 2023046445 (ebook) | ISBN 9781394160976 (hardback) | ISBN 9781394160990 (adobe pdf) | ISBN 9781394160983 (epub)
Subjects: LCSH: Leadership. | Industrial management.
Classification: LCC HD57.7 .C474 2024 (print) | LCC HD57.7 (ebook) | DDC 658.4/092—dc23/eng/20231005
LC record available at https://lccn.loc.gov/2023046444
LC ebook record available at https://lccn.loc.gov/2023046445

Cover Design: Wiley

SKY10062722_121423

Contents

Welcome

We believe you will find this book helpful, clear, concise, and most of all useful—as many, many other people have.

Substantial benefits are derived from using the Leadership Pipeline framework. Chief executives have told us that using the Leadership Pipeline accomplishes many things:

- Changes the dialogue at the executive table, focusing more on strategy and talent, not just revenue and profit

- Helps push accountability down the organization in a coherent way; frees those at the top to focus more on the future while lower levels drive productivity and early operating results

- Produces common standards for both performance and potential, differentiated by layer of leadership

- Inspires better coaching, given the improved clarity of expectations for all involved

- Provides a competitive advantage

- Serves as an invaluable resource for developing leaders at all levels

Human resources leaders have told us they now can do important work better:

- Focus coursework on the job to be done rather than on generic skills

- Anchor succession planning on what potential means and what it looks like

- Talk about people matters in a consistent way

- Have a framework for assessing and developing our own leadership talent

- Have leadership concepts that are enduring and simple enough that leaders at every level can quickly grasp what it means to be an effective leader

The overwhelmingly positive response to the first edition of *The Leadership Pipeline* (published in 2001) led to the second edition, published in 2011. Since the first edition, we have experienced an increasing interest in applying the Leadership Pipeline model. Our discussions with readers and our work as consultants have provided us with invaluable feedback about the model—feedback that has helped make this model even more effective in practice. We want to pass on the lessons we've learned so that companies can maximize the Pipeline's value.

Many of the best and most successful corporations in the world have adopted the Leadership Pipeline model as the core framework for their efforts on the human side of their businesses. CEOs and other senior executives at these leading companies tell us they have adopted the Leadership Pipeline because they believe it gives them the ability to stay ahead of their competition. Built on the common leadership "passages," it helps organizations select, develop, and assess leaders based on specific responsibilities and the required work values, time application, and skills at each leadership level—what we call the transition triad.

Our approach to the third edition of the book has been to make it even easier for organizations to implement the model and harvest the same benefits as those organizations already using it. The Leadership Pipeline model itself is timeless, but the business environment is ever changing. Organizational structures and business models evolve, and the macro trends in the surrounding world pull organizations in new directions. In this book, we both capture what has changed over the past years and look ahead to outline how best to use the model in the future.

Getting the Most out of This Book

Words and ideas mean different things to different people, more than ever in current society. You will get the most out of this book if you understand our words and ideas in the spirit and intent in which they were written. Here we define a few of the critical ones that are central to our book.

Leading Versus Managing

Distinguishing between leadership and management has been the subject to endless debate involving academics and practitioners. We find that discussion somewhat fruitless. At the end of the day, there is a job to be done in each leadership role that requires both. One doesn't work without the other. The right set of work values, time application, and skills include leading and managing.

In the first and second editions we consistently applied the term *manager*. In this edition we instead consistently apply the term *leader*. We changed the term to make it more palatable and more translatable. Most of the many languages this book has been translated into don't have a word for *manager*; they only have a word for *leader*.

Our point is: don't let yourself get hung up on these two terms while reading the book. Focus on what the leaders must deliver in their jobs and what it takes to deliver.

Roles Versus Hierarchy

We discuss and display the Leadership Pipeline in levels or layers. We are not defining a hierarchy or status. We are defining roles, packages of work to be done. It is possible for an individual to have three different roles at the same time. A person who reports to the chief executive and runs a business is the business leader. That person may have other leaders reporting (we call this leading leaders) and have individual contributors reporting to them (called leading others). We think it is important for that person to understand the requirements from all three roles. The role identification for any leadership role comes from the highest order of responsibility, such as business leader in this example.

Agility Versus Rigidity

There have been many ways of approaching business or organization success. Total Quality Management (TQM), matrix, lean, design thinking, and now agile are examples. Each of these operating models offer meaningful ways to improve productivity and performance. Terrific benefits have been derived in some cases. None of them are enough by themselves to run the entire enterprise. All enterprises require a foundation of basic activities that must be mastered. People have to be hired and developed, decisions have to be made about direction and resource allocation, plans are needed to put work in sequence, and so on no matter what operating model is chosen. We are offering the cradle or architecture in which any operating model, including agile, can sit.

Competencies Versus Work to Be Done

We have been invited into many organizations who have implemented competency models. Some of the common goals for their competency programs have been to strengthen leadership performance, improve daily dialogues on leadership, enable more accurate assessment of good leadership, and more reliable succession planning. The reason for inviting us in is always the same. After full implementation and a couple of years of hard work, the results were not sufficient. Many realize later that competencies work fine for skills training purposes, but not for performance assessment, or succession planning, or building a leader-led development culture.

The difficulty with competency models is very simple. Competencies represent "input" to performance—not actual performance. Also, they usually aren't differentiated; they are the same for every position even though the work is very different. Don't get us wrong, we do believe that it is important to have leadership competencies when you are in a leadership role. However, it remains input to performance and needs to be supported by other equally critical elements. In addition to skills, leaders need the right work values and the right time application.

The Leadership Pipeline model focuses on the job to be done and differentiates by layer. It focuses on what results they must deliver and what to do to deliver them.

In this third edition we will make it much easier for you to implement the core of the Leadership Pipeline without a detour for competency models or other partial solutions. For those who already have competency models in place, we will explain and give examples of how you can integrate competence frameworks in the Leadership Pipeline model without much dilution of the benefits of the Leadership Pipeline model or your competencies.

Who Should Read This Book

. . . Anyone who isn't a leader now but would like to become a leader

. . . Leaders who want to improve their leadership performance

. . . Talent or leadership development specialists who want to implement an enduring leadership development architecture, something that doesn't have to change every six months when a new idea surfaces or a new CEO or CHRO is appointed

. . . CEOs who want to make leadership development a competitive advantage

How to Read This Book

This book is divided into three sections.

The first section introduces you to the Leadership Pipeline and makes the business case for using it.

The second section defines differentiated leadership roles, emphasizing the work values, time application, and skills required to be successful in the role. To keep the leadership pipeline full and flowing, it's crucial that you are aware of the specific requirements, the common problems leaders experience in making a full transition into their role, and behaviors or attitudes that identify someone as having difficulty transitioning into the role.

The third section addresses some uses and applications to help you get the most from the model.

The pipeline is a very flexible model that organizations can adapt to their own situations and needs. It's also a model designed with changing leadership accountabilities in mind. Some of the traditional notions of what a leader needs to be and do are no longer valid.

To use the Leadership Pipeline approach effectively, you need to challenge traditional notions of leadership. You can't grow leaders unless you have an accurate development target, and this means acknowledging that the roles and responsibilities of leaders have shifted. The multilevel, multidimensional concept of leadership is a reality of modern business life. Once you start developing leaders with this new reality in mind, it will be that much easier to be effective in leadership development and talent management.

Finally, we would like to warn you away from a "mechanical" implementation of the Pipeline concept. In other words, push the model into your company and adapt it as needed. Do not push your company into the Pipeline model. We ask you to think holistically and with the complexity of people needs in mind.

The Leadership Pipeline model has proved to be a timeless tool for business success and is relevant for addressing the challenges of both today and tomorrow.

We trust that you will find this book delivers real value.

Enjoy the book!

Ram Charan: office@charanassoc.com
Stephen Drotter: sjdrotter@aol.com
Kent Jonasen: kent.jonasen@lp-institute.com
June 1, 2023

Introduction

Since it was first published, *The Leadership Pipeline* has provided a well-accepted set of principles and a framework for understanding the work of leaders. It defines the job to be done in key leadership roles and outlines the required skills to be applied, the appropriate allocation of their time, and the work they must value in order to be successful leaders.

The framework defines (1) how and why the work must be differentiated by role and (2) the requirements for transitioning from one role to the next. It has become a global standard for companies to use this framework to develop leaders and help them transition from one leadership role to another.

Hundreds of thousands of copies of the first and second edition of this book have been sold, and it has been printed in 12 different languages. Hundreds of organizations, for-profit and not-for-profit, have adopted its principles. Consulting firms use it to help their customers. Leaders and HR professionals tell us they use it in their everyday work. Business schools use it as course material. It has proven to be a timeless tool, applicable in every industry and geography.

Whereas the leadership-first principles in the Leadership Pipeline model stay the same, the leadership roles themselves are continuously influenced by external factors such as digitization,

COVID-19, increased employee leverage, and the global geopolitical uncertainty. Likewise, the leadership role is affected by adjusted business models and adjusted operating models.

Because most of these challenges are systemic—in other words, they affect every aspect of business—clear and consistent responses across the organization are needed. In particular, we must be clear about how leaders respond and it must be consistent across the organization. The one-liners and tag lines about leadership roles that seem to be everywhere won't cut it. They tend to be shallow and incomplete. *The Leadership Pipeline* offers a systemic approach that is deep and can be consistently applied across the entire organization to help you solve today's leadership challenges while at the same time preparing for tomorrow's challenges.

What This Update Offers

First, this edition helps leaders understand how the principles and framework apply in the current and likely future business environment. We are living in a period with incredible challenges for leaders in every aspect of life including business, politics, government, education, and religion. Perhaps the biggest challenge has come from *digitization*. Everybody has access to all or most of the data and information. Businesses are scrambling to find the best way to operate in this digital age, including where decisions will be made and who will make them. One set of challenges has come from steps taken to combat the COVID-19 pandemic. Many well-established leadership policies and practices were tipped over. Everyone one was vulnerable. Both of these challenges, digitization and COVID, have been complicated by a dramatic increase in *employee leverage*, especially for knowledge workers. Employees feel empowered to have their needs and interests met or they will quit and leave or quit and stay. Complaints on social media to the company's detriment are common. *Societal pressure* on a wide range of issues has put extreme pressure on organizations of all kinds to make changes in the way they operate and what leaders at all levels must focus on. All of these challenges are set in the context of *global uncertainty*. Climate change, jockeying for supremacy, war, inflation, population migration, and several other factors keep the world off balance. This uncertainty is likely to continue indefinitely.

Second, this update responds to those who've had difficulty in applying the model. Some can't find themselves in the model, some don't agree with what they find, some have misconceptions about what the model means, and some confuse bad personal experiences with the model being the problem rather than poor implementation being the problem. We would like to clear up these problems as best we can.

Third, this update seeks to reach leaders around the world who are not familiar with the Leadership Pipeline model but could benefit from knowing its principles and framework. Lots of people are reluctant to invest their time in an "old" leadership model because they fear it is outdated and not relevant now. By addressing current needs and giving *The Leadership Pipeline* a new birthday, we want to make its relevance for today's challenges clear and compelling.

Changing the Work of Leaders

There are always forces pushing on companies, employees, and the work itself. Since our last update there have been several major forces causing leaders to rethink what they do and what they ask others to do. Here is our view of the most powerful forces affecting leaders now.

Digitization: Everyone Has the Data

Technology has changed how we work, when we work, what we work on, where we work, what we work with, and whom we work with. It has also changed the speed with which we work and the volume of work we can accomplish in a workday. These changes can only be described as sweeping and it is unlikely we will ever go back. If anything, this change is accelerating. We are now squarely in the digital age. Digitization is a continuous process, not an event. We can expect an increase in applications and use. Artificial intelligence is growing rapidly and nobody knows what the impact will be. As a result, some basic chores for leaders have changed so new ways of developing leaders are needed now.

The availability of data at lower organization levels and the speed at which it is accumulated has changed the balance of decision-making. Information that used to be available only to the top leaders is now at everyone's fingertips. Lower-level leaders and the manage-self population are in a position to make increasingly more important decisions. Transparency of the organization's situation has increased so it is harder to mislead people.

The work of leaders has to account for the impact of technology and digitization on the organization and the people. Decision-making authority must be passed down to lower levels to take full advantage of their capability. Those decisions include more than work time and location. Critically important business matters such as profit and pricing can be handled at much lower levels because the required information is available there. More emphasis on development and coaching with less on control helps those at lower levels use their information power and decision-making authority appropriately for business success. More negotiation and less command help keep motivation at a high level. Increased engagement through soliciting new ideas and being open to them is a core requirement.

COVID-19: Everyone Who Can Works from Home

COVID-19 presented an enormous risk that required an extreme response. Everyone who could was required to work from home, and technology and digitization made that possible. Many subsequently examined their values and decided to give higher priority to work/life balance and time with family. Many, many people liked working from home and now don't want to commute to their offices or at least only be in the office a few days a week. Organizations are having a hard time getting them to come to the office. The hybrid organization, with some at home and some in the office, and never at the same time, seems to be here to stay. There are some benefits to the hybrid organization and some important challenges as well. Without judging the merits of working from home or working from the office, it has made the leaders' role more difficult. Building teamwork, maintaining the company culture, managing performance, building relationships, driving engagement, and coaching now require different skills.

To make hybrid organizations work, leaders' time application will have to shift toward frequent one-on-one engagement. Communication, team-building, check-ins, culture maintenance, and so on with a team that sits in different geographic locations has been a challenge for some time. Anecdotal evidence suggests it has seldom been done effectively. Now it has to become a true skill even in small domestic companies. Leaders must value the remote and the in-office team members equally.

Employee Leverage: They Tell You What They Want and You Better Listen

New generations are growing up with internet and social media as dominant forces in their lives. Carrying a hand-held computer has been an everyday experience since grammar school. As a result, there are many distinctive attributes that must be understood and acknowledged.

These workers have incredible skills in using technology. Speedy access to all kinds of information coupled with processing power puts them far ahead of previous generations. This access gives them knowledge power and their skills are in demand. They are informed enough to know, and we think rightfully so, that they want jobs that have intrinsic value. They want to contribute, learn new skills, and make a difference in some way. Peripheral jobs of little value to them or the business will cause them to go elsewhere. They have the communication platforms to let the world know what it's like to work in your company. Because things are moving fast they don't want to stay in a job too long. They want feedback on how they are doing and coaching to enhance their development so they can move up. Work/life integration is more important than ever and burnout has become a major topic of discussion.

The Great Resignation presented businesses with shortages of key skills. First, the concern was that people simply left the job market for good. However, workforce participation has largely returned post-COVID but shortages of key skills and service workers remain high. People still quit large-scale organizations to pursue other work arrangements that give them more control. Even with the current reduction in tech industry jobs, critical shortages are expected to continue and thus put much more pressure on retention. These challenges—attracting, developing, and retaining talent—have been around for quite a while. What is new is the availability of alternatives for employees and their willingness to choose them.

The most obvious response to these challenges is improving the leadership quality within the organization: not by acquiring perceived better leaders from other companies but by systematically improving leadership skills and the leadership agenda across the organization. Leaders need to address expectations of meaningful work, conduct dialogues with employee about their needs, and manage employees' personal growth to facilitate recruitment and increase retention. A meaningful job supported by any needed coaching now is the anchor point. Offering a better, more defined future with managed development is a source of competitive advantage or competitive disadvantage if done poorly. More time allocated to this work by all leaders at every level and more employee involvement are required.

Societal Pressure: More Than Profit Is Expected

Activism on a wide range of issues has put significant pressure on organizations of all kinds to make changes in the way they operate. Today, businesses and other organizations are pressured to concern themselves with climate change and the environment, diversity and inclusion, governance, equity in pay and promotions, gender issues, the impact of a pandemic, droughts, citizenship, and other societal issues. Leadership at all levels is now required to look at decision-making through these new lenses for production, allocation of resources and rewards, hiring and promotions, workforce composition, and community involvement.

The point of the pressure is to force change in institutions of all kinds. Leaders at every level have to play a part in taking charge of the changes. The pressure creates internal conflict, which leaders must resolve. Which one should be our priority today? How should resources be deployed? What has to get fixed or changed? Who should be promoted? Enterprise-level policies and programs are put in place to address some of these. How they translate on the ground is determined by local leaders. Decisions made on a daily basis determine the effectiveness of the organization's response to societal issues. Taking time to think through choices and their affect is a critical part of a leader's role. Valuing the needed change is the key.

Geopolitical Uncertainty: Look at What Just Happened, What Should Be Done About It?

Continuous major events across the globe are putting pressure on the senior leadership roles. Yesterday, common sense was running your business one way; today, it is running it in a different way, and tomorrow will bring a new common sense. We can exemplify this with current events.

The very different ways that countries dealt with the COVID-19 pandemic significantly influenced how international companies needed to think about their supply chain. Sources closer to home or at home are critical. Also, this pandemic exemplified how fast consumer habits can change and that the changes can stick.

Shortly after the Russian/Ukraine war began, many Western companies left Russia. Concern about having production capability for critical products that sit mainly outside a country's border has led to many changes in Asia. As hard as those changes were, it was the easy part. Completely rethinking supply chains and establishing new production facilities is a much harder leadership challenge.

New Business Models: Partners Needed

The old days of being self-sufficient and going it alone are over. No company can do everything itself. It is increasingly about creating an ecosystem by building partnerships. Some partnerships will create new or greater value for your customers. Some will give you new technology and new core competencies. Some will help you interface better with regulators

What will your constellation look like? How do you build it? And, more important, how do you manage it? This way of operating has created a new job for many senior executives. They need to be ecosystem builders. Many companies in the future, if they aren't already, will be platform companies. Platforms require building an ecosystem. For many leaders, new skills will be required for working effectively with partners. It can be complicated, particularly when there is more than one partner.

The Independent Workforce: A New Balancing Act for Preserving the Culture

Independent work is booming these days. More and more people abandon the traditional employer-employee relationship to be part of the gig economy. Drivers, programmers, designers, home health care, coaches, and many other kinds of workers comprise a large and growing self-directed workforce. This trend certainly represents an opportunity for organizations because they can more easily scale up and down as needed. Maintaining the right culture while achieving needed production from independent workers, who are mixing with the full-time core of people, requires explicit tasks and performance standards defined by the leaders.

Another challenge is that independent workers don't come and go at the organizations' demand. Many questions arise: How do you attract and retain these independent workers? What are they requesting from their direct manager—how is it different from what full-time employees request? There is thoughtful planning required to navigate the staffing needs, employee needs, and contractor scheduling to get the work done.

New Organization Structures: Enabling Knowledge Worker Productivity

Much of the work to be done now is knowledge work. Knowledge worker productivity has not been sufficiently addressed in the past. Businesses have adopted a more fluid approach to organizing, at least in part, to make knowledge workers more productive. Matrices, agile teams, flatter structures, evolving roles, delegation of authority enable knowledge workers to adapt more quickly to changing requirements. Removing bureaucracy, increasing decision-making authority, shortening communication lines, better use of resources, and creating multifunctional teams have all become common practices. A person can be a team leader today and a team member tomorrow. Moving from leading a team of people in the same function one day to leading a multifunctional team the next has become commonplace. Sharing authority and accountability with other leaders from other organizations requires compromise and flexibility not needed in the past.

Traditional reporting lines are superseded on a regular basis. Leaders at higher layers need to value "what's good for the business" rather than just "what's good for my function." At much lower levels the give-and-take can be a daily exercise. One anchor point that makes this fluctuation possible is having clear goals developed collaboratively. Expressing goals as external results such as "reducing response time to customer requests" rather than internal "meeting our schedule" helps to create common purpose. Because confusion is likely to be rampant, role definitions are especially important.

We will talk more about the impact of new structures in Chapter 11.

Solving the Problems of Today and Tomorrow

The hot new ideas in almost every industry—fashion, politics, food, health, social media, and so on—get tremendous attention, and the "older ideas" get overlooked. Leadership isn't any different in that regard. New books, new models, new gurus, and the like pop up with great frequency and capture the imagination of many. Whether they have value is another matter altogether. The most reliable test is time, not popularity.

We are concerned that if today's leaders are caught up in new ideas, they won't learn about the Leadership Pipeline. They might think because it's "old" it isn't relevant. But the fact is that the Leadership Pipeline has continuously helped leaders for decades. Once implemented, it remains the backbone of organizations' leadership frameworks. It holds up over time because it represents a set of leadership-first principles—things that don't change. These principles can be applied in most situations today because they are helpful in addressing the leadership-related elements of today's problems and opportunities.

As of this writing, mid-2023, some of today's problems include the following:

- The Great Resignation

- Difficulty retaining key employees

- Silent quitting

- Difficulty "producing" sufficient talent

- Assimilating remote workers and making hybrid organizations work

- Transitioning to digitization

- Maintaining an appropriate culture

- Creating a safe workplace

- Ensuring diversity and inclusion

- Maintaining equitable pay and opportunities

- Burnout

These problems are all leadership problems. They are most often caused by leaders not being told in a hands-on language what success looks like in their leadership role. Many never have support in transitioning fully into their new roles. The transition triad—the appropriate set of skills, work values, and time application—are not usually arrived at intuitively. Explanation and discussion are necessary. That is the core of what the Leadership Pipeline does. Time will not outgrow this need. Plus, as the work environment gets even more complicated, the list of problems will grow. Learning the Leadership Pipeline principles is the best way to develop leaders ready to tackle whatever tomorrow brings.

Applying the Leadership Pipeline Model

We have spoken with many business leaders and human resource (HR) executives who embraced the Leadership Pipeline model on their own—but then were met with resistance in parts of their organization when trying to implement it.

There seem to be two root causes of this. One derives from misconceptions of what the Leadership Pipeline model really is. We'll address those misconceptions in the next section, "Dispelling Myths About the Model." The other root cause is that some colleagues resist because they had bad experiences in previous companies where the model was poorly implemented. Because they didn't know it was poorly implemented, they just blamed the model. So we wanted to clarify a few points.

Perhaps the most important thing to understand about using the Leadership Pipeline is that it isn't meant to be the *answer* to anything. It's an evidence-based set of first-leadership principles that helps you design your own leadership framework and Leadership Portrait for each key leadership role in your organization. It isn't telling you how exactly to organize. It isn't a career model. The principles are meant to help you select, develop, and assess the performance of leaders at all levels. Improving the effectiveness of leaders and making sure all the necessary leadership work is being done are two of the many benefits of implementing the Pipeline model.

Another angle of this is the fact that, when we first designed the model, we didn't think that specifics about *how* to apply it would be as necessary as they've proven to be. We also couldn't possibly have anticipated and dreamed up solutions to all the sorts of scenarios companies face. Today, because we've received many questions from and talked with many organizations, we have a much clearer sense of what's needed when applying the model. Our updated explanations on how to apply the framework concepts in many different situations is thus an important part of this new edition.

We will address application in part by much more explicitly describing and illustrating the Leadership Pipeline model—as well as how to operationalize the model. Furthermore, we have added a dedicated chapter on implementation strategies. You'll find all this in Part III of this book.

Dispelling Myths About the Model

We mentioned previously there are misconceptions about what the Leadership Pipeline model really is. It's only natural that myths have developed over the 20 years since the book was first pub-lished. We frequently help companies address these myths. We want to dispel these myths.

Myth 1: We don't have six *leadership* layers in our organization, so we can't apply the Leadership Pipeline model.

Our response: Some people read the entire Leadership Pipeline book, others read the chapters they found relevant for them, but many these days just Google Leadership Pipeline and read brief reviews and look at graphical illustrations. The consequence of the last has been that many people identify the Leadership Pipeline model only with the illustration of its original leadership passages (see Figure 0.1).

However, this illustration is not the Leadership Pipeline model itself. It is merely an illustration of some of the most common leadership roles and most common leadership transitions. The Leadership Pipeline is actually a set of first principles that you can use in any type of organization to map key leadership roles, define the job to be done, and outline the required work values, time application, and skills. If your company only has two layers, then your pipeline only has two layers. The top layer has more to do than simply leading others. We discuss what should happen with some of the necessary work in later chapters.

We encourage you to study Chapter 1 to get your mind around the model. In Chapters 3 through 7, we bring the model alive by giving specific examples of leadership roles. Please keep in mind that you may find leadership roles within your organization that are not directly covered in this book. But you can apply the Leadership Pipeline model to describe these roles yourself.

Myth 2: The model is hierarchical.

Our response: This is yet another myth growing out of the perception that the leadership passage illustration in Figure 0.1 is

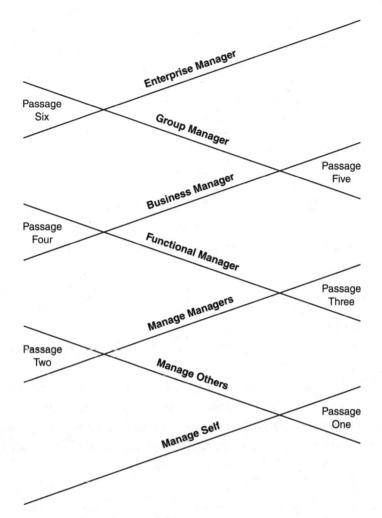

Figure 0.1. Based on a short paper called "Critical Career Crossroads" written by Walter R. Mahler in 1978.

itself the Leadership Pipeline model. In reality, the Leadership Pipeline model is anything but a hierarchical model. Actually, many companies use the Leadership Pipeline model to break down hierarchies!

Titles and company layers represent hierarchy. The Leadership Pipeline, however, is a role-based model. It does not look at your title because titles can be misleading. It looks at the job to be done.

As an example, you will find that many function leaders have both those who lead others (leaders-of-others) and those who lead leaders (leaders-of-leaders) reporting to them. Sometimes, high-level specialists (those who lead themselves) also report to them. From a hierarchical perspective, all direct reports to the functional leader are at the same organizational layer. But their leadership roles are completely different and the leadership requirements are different. Organizations not applying the Leadership Pipeline model usually end up with a hierarchical approach to select, develop, and assess leaders. They use titles or other status indicators to make distinctions, not job content. Whereas, if you apply the Leadership Pipeline model, you would recognize that it is not the reporting line that is the critical parameter in developing leaders and assessing leadership performance. It is the leadership job to be done. The leadership job to be done is differentiated by leadership roles—not leadership hierarchy.

Myth 3: The model defines a common career path for leaders.

Our response: Once again, if only looking at the illustration in Figure 0.1 and not reading even one chapter in *The Leadership Pipeline*, we can appreciate that it looks like you have to follow a certain career path. But, again, that is not the purpose of this illustration. Not all roles exist in all parts of organizations. In finance and HR, for example, many people move from leading-others roles straight to the function leader role simply because there may not be any leading-leaders roles within the functions. Many business leaders were never functional leaders before moving into the business leader role. They may have grown up in the commercial or operations side of the business and then moved to a country manager role. From there they went to a regional manager role and then finally to the business leader role. Also, careers aren't usually linear. Some people move back and forth between a specialist role, a leading-others role, and a project leader role. Only a few people end up in a function or business leader role because there are only a few of them. There is nothing wrong with that. For most people, function leader and business leader roles are not a goal. The value of our model comes from making explicit the skills that must be acquired, how time should be applied, and the work that must be valued in order to make a transition successfully—whatever transition it is.

Myth 4: This is only for large organizations.

Our response: Smaller companies get better use from this model than bigger ones. Smaller companies that are growing often outgrow their structures and need to add leadership roles. What most often stands in the way for smaller companies growing bigger is failure to do so. Our model provides them with ideas and definitions of what roles to add and where. As companies grow, preparing for the future becomes more important. Anticipating and avoiding obstacles to prevent losing what has been achieved becomes a new leadership requirement. The person at the very top has to evolve their role by moving up the pipeline. Bigger companies frequently have more financial cushion for absorbing the shocks of the market. They also have more leadership cushion in the form of more leaders, as well as better system and processes to help with growth. They generally can withstand a few weak leaders. Smaller companies can't. They have to get the leadership work right.

There are many other myths and misinterpretations. We will try to identify and address them as we progress through. The message we are trying to deliver is not one of rigidity. Rather, we are trying to convey a body of requirements for success of any organization. It is just easier and more understandable if we break the material into some logical set of pieces. It isn't the Leadership Pipeline model that defines your organization structure. The size of your organization, as measured by number of products or headcount or revenue or geography or all four, defines the likely shape of your structure. The Leadership Pipeline model is the perpetual source for addressing leadership challenges, independent of what organizational design you have chosen.

PART I

WHY THE LEADERSHIP
PIPELINE MATTERS

1

Leadership Pipeline Overview

To get value from the Leadership Pipeline you have to understand its basics. This concise overview is meant to give you easy access to the timeless tool ideas, principles, and framework. It is the place to start if you want to build a pipeline of leaders that is full and flowing; the Leadership Pipeline is a timeless tool for business success. More in-depth treatment of the various elements is covered in subsequent chapters as well as some applications.

The Big Ideas

The Leadership Pipeline model is based on a set of ideas developed from assessments for over 1,500 leaders who were candidates for CEO, business general manager, CFO, and other C-suite positions in a wide range of industries. These assessments are composed of a four-hour interview tracing the person's career, achievements, and skill development. Findings are validated with the relevant boss and others who have hard data.

This assessment data has been combined with an applied ongoing research project, conducted since 2010. In structured workshops more than 15,000 leaders at different leadership levels have participated in discussions. These discussions focused on the challenges they faced when moving into a new leadership level.

In Chapters 3 through 6 we share the results of that research for each leadership role.

The model has proven to be universally applicable and able to withstand the test of time. We have seen very few organizations discontinue using the model once it has been implemented. Whereas most leadership models don't survive even one CEO change, the Leadership Pipeline model survives one change after another.

We have learned there is no such thing as the right organization structure for any organization. The Leadership Pipeline doesn't describe any particular organization or business and we certainly are not recommending that you use it that way. Rather, it is a framework that any organization or business can use as a starting point for building its own operating structure. Digitization is changing the way business works so flexibility is essential. If you use this framework, adapting to changing requirements is easier. The process for developing leaders becomes clearer, specifically, what must be developed, when to develop it, and whom to develop.

Five principles define the Leadership Pipeline model:

Leadership work must be clearly defined and differentiated by layer/role. Because there is so much leadership work to be done it has to be divided up to be sure everything required is assigned. Overlap is counterproductive. Today's challenges are like a magnet drawing everyone's attention. Working on the future suffers or isn't done at all.

The effectiveness of leaders is complex and must be understood in at least three dimensions: required skills, how time is applied, and the appropriate work values. A leader's job, like any other, is composed of a set of tasks. To accomplish these tasks basic skills are required. Knowing the skills required has been understood in at least general terms for 100 years. There is an important obstacle that hasn't been well understood. Even though leaders are skilled, they only apply those skills when they truly start valuing leadership work and appreciate how they uniquely create value as leaders. Many leaders behave as if their leadership work comes on top of their job rather than being their job. Operational matters and doing things themselves dominate their time schedule. They struggle freeing up time for leadership.

When leaders change organization layer/role, a significant transition is required. The different leadership layers/roles are completely different jobs. Leaving behind the work values, time application, and skills required by the previous layer/role is necessary. Understanding and adopting new ones appropriate to the new layer/role is a difficult and critical condition for success. Doing the work of the lower layer/role while failing to adopt the requirements of the new layer/role is destructive to the organization and a leading cause of leadership failure.

For sustained business success a pipeline of leaders that is full and flowing is a fundamental requirement. The flow of leaders is critically important. There is never enough effective leadership. Many of the current business problems, such as quiet quitting, burnout, the Great Resignation, isolation, and so on, are leadership failures. When new leaders are needed for any reason, filling leadership positions quickly with high confidence is the most desirable condition. Flow matters but is hindered by many things. The worst impediment comes from those who work at the wrong level.

It is the collective effectiveness of all leaders that determines an organization's success, not the brilliance of a few. Many companies invest heavily in developing leaders but are not satisfied with the results. On examination, they are developing 50 leaders and ignoring 200 others. In our experience, there is little value in developing only the "stars." There is an interdependence among leaders that goes up, down, and sideways. Common expectations about what leaders will do and how they will do it, supported with appropriate development, provide the basis for collaboration and teamwork.

If goods or services have to be produced and people are involved, a leader is necessary to keep production moving. That leader will set direction, engage the team, support team members, make decisions, allocate resources, and measure progress at a minimum. Therefore, Leadership Pipeline principles and ideas apply. All but the tiniest of organizations can benefit from using it.

With these principles in place, applying the Leadership Pipeline model will help you in the following:

- Mapping typical leadership roles and passages across the organization

- Defining the job to be done for these leadership roles across the organization

- Defining the critical transitions in terms of work values, time application, and skills that leaders face when moving to new leadership roles

The Core Leadership Passages

When you design your own Leadership Pipeline framework, you will benefit from using the five core leadership passages as the starting point. What makes them core building blocks is most organizations need at least three and probably four of them. Even small organizations usually have three of them. They are needed to cover both working on the present and working on the future. Furthermore, in most companies 95% of leadership roles are either exactly one of these five roles or they are a close variation/combination of the roles in some shape.

The five roles are expressed as passages. Moving from one to the next is a major event in the life of a leader. It represents a significant transition that can't be learned in a day or by taking a generalized leadership course. Our goal here is to help you become familiar with the work values, time application, and skills demanded by each passage. Once you grasp what they entail and the challenges involved in making each transition from one to the next, you will be better able to use this information to unclog your organization's pipeline and facilitate your own growth as a leader. The five chapters in Part II of this book will provide you with in-depth information, ideas, and tools for achieving full performance at all levels in your organization.

As you read about each passage, you will naturally apply it to your own organization and question how we define and divide each one. The odds are you will think of at least one (and possibly more) transitions in your company that has not been addressed in Figure 1.1. And this is exactly what we hope for. The purpose of detailing the passages is to equip you to work actively with the model rather than just applying it as it is. Each organization is unique, and each probably has at least one, and larger organizations two, leadership transitions with distinctive aspects.

As you become more attuned to each passage we believe you'll see how they apply to your own situation and organization. If there is a transition phase in your business or organization that doesn't fit this model, create your own definition and tell us about it. (Our email addresses are at the end of the Welcome.) It might be helpful to others. We illustrate our updated model in Figure 1.1.

Passage 1: Leading Others

New, young employees usually spend their first few years with the organization as an individual contributor. Whether they are in engineering or sales or finance their skill requirements are technical or professional. They contribute by doing the assigned work within a given time frame and in ways that meet objectives. By sharpening and broadening their individual skills they make increased contributions. They are then considered to be promotable. From a time

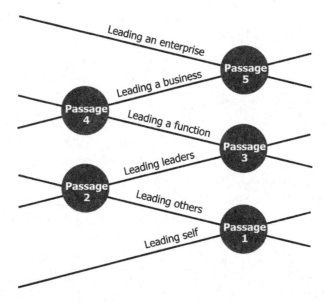

Figure 1.1. The Five Key Leadership Roles and Turns Illustrated.
Source: Based on Walter Mahler's "Critical Career Crossroads," revised by
Stephen Drotter.

application standpoint, their learning involves planning so they
can deliver on schedule, punctuality so they show up for work and
meetings on time, and checking their work to ensure quality and
reliability. The work values to be developed include accepting the
company culture (values) and adopting appropriate professional
standards. When people become skilled individual contributors
who produce good results—especially when they demonstrate an
ability to collaborate with others—they usually receive additional
responsibilities or more complex work. When they demonstrate
the ability to handle these new responsibilities and adhere to the
company's values, they are often promoted to the first line of
leadership.

When this happens, they are at the beginning of passage 1.
Though this may seem like an easy, natural progression, many
new managers trip. The highest performing individuals are often
reluctant to give up what they were doing. They want to keep

doing the things that made them successful. As a result, many first-time leaders take the new title, status, and money but don't make the transition. They become leaders without accepting the requirements.

The skills that new leaders have to learn include planning work for their team (not just themselves), choosing new teammates, assigning work, teaching new hires, monitoring progress, coaching, and measuring the output. First-line leaders need to learn how to allocate their time to help others perform effectively. They cannot allocate all their time to handling tasks themselves, putting out fires and taking advantage of opportunities. They must shift from doing work to getting work done through others.

Reallocating time is an especially difficult transition requirement for first-time leaders. Part of the problem is that many neophyte leaders still prefer to spend time on their "old" work, even as they take charge of a group of people. The pressure to spend less time on individual work and more time managing will increase at each passage. If people don't start making changes in how they allocate their time right from the beginning, they are bound to become liabilities if they move up. It is a major reason pipelines clog.

The most difficult change for new managers to make at passage 1 involves work values. Specifically, they need to start valuing managerial work, not just tolerating it. They must believe that making time for others, planning for others, coaching, and the like are necessary tasks and their responsibility. More than that, they must view other-directed work as mission critical to their own success. For instance, first-line leaders in the financial services industry find this transition extremely difficult. The industry values production and producers. New leaders must learn to value making their people good producers. Given that these values had nothing to do with their success so far it is difficult for them to make this dramatic shift in what they view as meaningful. Although changes in skills and time application are visible and measurable, changes in work values are hard to assess. Someone may appear to have the right values when their boss is watching but they haven't really changed. Because changes in work values are hard to make, they frequently require upper management reinforcement.

Mindset has been a critical but undervalued performance driver. It gives the first-line manager the starting point for each day. Individual contributors should start each day with "delivering excellence" as their mindset. The desire to perform their tasks to the best of their ability today and every day sets them up for success. The first-line leader is the frontline for delivering results. It could be offense or defense that is needed; they have to deliver it. Changes conceived from on high could include cutting costs or speeding up delivery or becoming agile. These must be first delivered at the frontline. The required mindset is "take charge, help the team, and be flexible."

Passage 2: Leading Leaders

This leadership passage is frequently ignored compared to the previous one, where the transition requirements are more obvious. Few companies address this passage directly in their training even though this level is where a company's management foundation is constructed. Leaders in this second passage—leaders-of-leaders—select and develop the first-line leaders; some will eventually become the company's senior leaders.

Perhaps the biggest difference from the previous passage is that here leaders must focus on leadership work only. They are now two layers removed from delivery of products or services. As leaders-of-others they may well have had some production tasks to perform or teach through demonstration. Now they have to select leaders, people who are at passage 1. They have to assign leadership work to them, train and develop them as leaders, measure their progress, and coach for improvement. This is also the point where they start to think beyond their own unit and start to consider how best to connect with other units that support the overall business.

All of this is hard to do if they still value individual contributions and technical work to the exclusion of everything else. Too often people who are promoted to passage 2 have skipped passage 1. They were promoted to first-line leader but didn't change work values, time application, skills, or mindset. As a result they clog the leadership pipeline because they hold first-line leaders accountable for technical or professional work rather than leadership work. Because they themselves skipped the first passage and still value individual contribution above leadership results, they poison the leadership well. They maintain and even instill the wrong values in those individuals reporting to them. They usually choose high-achieving technical experts for first-line leadership positions rather than true potential leaders. They are unwilling or unable to differentiate between those who can do and those who can lead.

Leaders at passage 2 need to be able to identify values-based resistance to leadership work, which is a common reaction among first-line leaders. Leaders-of-leaders need to recognize that the software design engineer who would rather design software than lead others to develop software cannot be allowed to move up to leadership work. No matter how brilliant they might be at design, they become obstacles in the leadership pipeline if they derive no job satisfaction from leading people. In fact, one of the tough responsibilities of leaders-of-leaders is to return leaders-of-others to individual contributor roles if they don't shift their work values, time application, and skills.

Coaching new first-line leaders on how to lead is essential because so many new leaders don't receive any formal training. They are dependent on their boss for instruction on the job. Coaching requires time to go through the instruction-performance-feedback cycle repeatedly until the performance is evident. Some and perhaps many leaders aren't willing to allocate their time in this way. In many organizations coaching isn't rewarded and its absence isn't recognized. No wonder new leaders-of-leaders don't think it is mission critical.

Mindset has to make a major shift. The "take charge, help the team, and be flexible" orientation has some value at this level but there are bigger issues that must be the starting point each day. They make the work flow among units run by their direct report and between their organization and other parts of the business where their work comes from and where it goes. They also connect the bottom of the organization where the operating work is done to the strategic part of their business. Information from these connections enables them to create a context for their people. The required mindset is "connections and context." The absence of connections and context makes organizations seem and feel chaotic in addition to being unproductive.

Passage 3: Leading a Function

This transition is tougher than it seems. On the surface both leaders-of-leaders and function leaders lead leaders and make connections with other parts of the business. Lurking under the surface are some major challenges. To communicate with the individual contributors they have to penetrate two layers before they reach the intended audience. New communication skills are needed. Inevitably this new layer requires the function leader to take charge of parts of the organization where they have little or no experience. Learning this new (to them) work and learning to value it at the same time can be a challenge. At the same time, function leaders report to business leaders and are part of the business team. Now, they have to take into consideration the needs, programs, roles, and challenges of the other functions. Two major transitional skills are team play with other functions and competition for resources based on business needs.

Perhaps the most difficult transition for new function leaders is moving from operational work to developing and implementing function strategy. Blending their strategy with the overall business strategy, with all the give-and-take involved, is a real challenge. From a time application standpoint, that means participating in business meetings and working with the other functions, which takes away from their time for function work. In light of this time requirement, delegation of major function tasks to their direct reports is the only way to get everything done well.

This leadership passage requires an increase in maturity. In one sense maturity means thinking and acting like a function leader, not like a function member. It also means adopting a broad, long-term perspective. Long-term strategy requires state-of-the-art thinking, futuristic thinking for the function for understanding and building competitive advantage. It is usually what gives these leaders the most trouble. Function strategy that enables the business to do something better than competition may give the business a short-term advantage. Long-term sustainable advantage is the objective—not just a temporary edge.

The following case study illustrates the challenges new function managers face.

Case study

Six months ago, Tom was named director of plant operations. In this capacity he has five direct reports: four who run large assembly facilities and one who runs purchasing of components. Although Tom's experiences have helped him appreciate sales, finance, and other functions, Tom has trouble with planning beyond the function's immediate requirements and with keeping in touch with individual contributors who are doing delicate assembly of hi-tech products. Not only is it difficult for Tom to define the steps necessary for the facilities to become a more integrated assembly operation but also he has lost touch with technicians he knew from previous lower-level assignments. They had been a source of invaluable real-time information he could use in making plans.

At many organizations, a guy like Tom could muddle through and his strengths would compensate for his weaknesses, at least on the surface. But on closer inspection, we can see that Tom isn't a full performer at this new layer. For instance, it's important that Tom build skills in skip-level communication. He needs to know, without diminishing the authority of the plant managers who report to him, what individual contributors are working on and how well the processes are working. If he doesn't develop this skill, he will run the risk of alienating the plant managers and first-line managers. Luckily, Tom's company has an assessment program in place that identified his struggle with passage 3 and is providing coaching and the opportunity to attend a first-rate executive development program that will help him build the necessary skills for this leadership level.

Transitioning to passage 3 requires a "strategic leadership" mindset. Adopting that mindset is almost impossible without developing strategic planning and thinking skills. Clearly, strategy training from the boss or from outsiders should be part of any transition effort. Without it, success will be superficial at best. Promoting the "best engineer" to be the function leader of engineering has always been an iffy proposition.

Passage 4: Leading a Business

Most business leaders tell us this is their favorite of all positions they have held. They are usually given significant autonomy, which those with leadership and entrepreneurial instincts relish. They have all the key functions on their team and can see the results of their effort in the marketplace.

This transition is reported to be the most challenging of their career. This is a very sharp turn; a major shift in work values, time application, skills, and mindset is required. It's not simply a matter of becoming more strategic and cross-functional, though it is important to continue developing these abilities rooted in the previous passage. Now they are in charge of integrating the functions, whereas previously they simply had to understand and work with the other functions. But the biggest shift is from looking at plans or proposals functionally (can we do it professionally, technically, or physically?) to looking at them from a profit perspective (will we make any money if we do this?) and to a long-term view (is the profit sustainable?). New business leaders must fundamentally change the way they think.

There are probably more new and unfamiliar responsibilities here than at any other level. For those who worked in only one function for their entire career a business manager position represents unexplored territory. They have suddenly become responsible for unfamiliar functions and outcomes. Not only do they have to learn to lead new functions but also they must become skilled at working with a wider range of people than ever before. They need to become sensitive to function differences; they must learn to communicate clearly and effectively with new audiences.

One of the most challenging aspects of this new layer is the balancing act between future goals and current needs—making trade-offs between short-term and long-term goals, and between the functions for resource allocation. Meeting quarterly (or monthly) profit, market share, product, and people targets while at the same time planning for goals three to five years into the future is a stretch. The paradox of balancing short-term and long-term thinking is one that bedevils leaders at this passage—and why one of the critical needs is having sufficient thinking time. At this level leaders need to stop "doing" and reserve time for reflection and analysis.

When business leaders don't make this turn completely the pipeline becomes severally clogged. For example, a common failure at this level is not valuing staff functions. Directing and integrating finance, human resources, legal, and other support functions are crucial business manager responsibilities. When leaders don't understand or value support staff, these employees don't deliver full performance. When the business leaders belittle or diminish their roles, staff people deliver half-hearted effort and become energy drainers. Business leaders must learn to take advice, accept feedback, and trust the staff functions. Business leaders who do so find they have more time to think.

The required mindset is a major transition from the previous layer. In simple terms, an effective view of this role is "profitable leadership." Every dollar spent should add value, so valuing one function over others leads to poor performance and decreases the return on salary. Exciting new projects must have a return on investment. Innovation often leads to increased profit. This mindset helps the new business leaders move away from activity and toward the bottom line.

Passage 5: Leading an Enterprise

The transition required for the fifth passage is more focused on values than skills. To an even greater extent, people making this transition must reinvent their self-concept as an enterprise leader. To be effective as the leader of the institution, long-term visionary thinking is required. At the same time they must develop operating mechanisms to know and drive quarter-by-quarter performance that is in tune with longer strategy. The trade-offs involved can be mind-bending, and enterprise leaders learn to value these decisions. In addition, this new leadership role often requires well-developed external sensitivities—and the ability to manage external constituencies, sense significant external shifts, and do something about them before they affect the enterprise. They value this outward-looking perspective.

Enterprise leaders need to come to terms with the fact that their performance will be based on three or four high-leverage decisions annually; they must set those three or four mission-critical priorities and focus on them. There's a subtle but fundamental shift from strategic to visionary thinking and from a business to a global perspective. There is also a letting-go process that should take place if it hasn't previously. Enterprise leaders must let go of the pieces (as in individual products and customers) and focus on the whole (as in the conception, development, production, and marketing of all products to all customers).

At this level an enterprise leader, commonly called CEO, must assemble a team of high-achieving and ambitious direct reports, knowing that some of them want the CEO job but choosing them for the team anyway. This is the only leadership position in the organization for which inspiring the entire employee population through a variety of communication tools is essential.

When the leadership pipeline gets clogged at the top, it negatively affects all leadership levels. A CEO who has skipped one or more passages can diminish the performance not only of the team that reports directly but also of individuals all the way down the line. Such a CEO not only fails to develop other leaders but also fails to fulfill the responsibilities that come with the position.

Preparation for the CEO role cannot be taken lightly. The role is one of a kind in the enterprise, so no direct preparation is possible. But a proven route is to take on a variety of positions that provide different challenges, both operational and strategic. Some accountability for external relationship building is also useful. Preparation has to start well beforehand, and several people have to be preparing simultaneously. The failure rate for enterprise leaders is higher than most other positions. Frequently, the new enterprise leader doesn't realize how significant the transition is, so they don't pay enough attention to their own development.

Defining the Job to Be Done

Understanding and addressing these transitions is critical for making leaders successful. We think it is also necessary to understand the job that must be done by each leadership role. We spell it out in this book for the five most common roles. Leadership work is not all the same, but many companies operate with one set of leadership competencies or principles or values for all leaders. That doesn't seem to work very well. Value creation by leaders varies as their roles get bigger or they have more resources to address. Therefore, the leadership job to be done is different. In addition to clarifying the work to be done for five leadership roles, we also identify some likely activities or tasks required to be successful. Figure 1.2 provides a visual for leaders-of-others. (We revisit this in Chapter 3, where you'll see this figure again.)

The first column, **The Work**, defines the basic leadership work that is to be carried out by the leadership role. This template should be used to help leaders focus on the important job elements. Our choice of words is deliberate and consistent so we

The Work	Required Activities
Set direction	• Clearly define the roles and priorities of direct reports. • Create a clear understanding of how direct reports' personal business objectives tie into overall team and business-unit objectives. • Engage direct reports in establishing personal business objectives.
Empower	• Enable direct reports to deal effectively with their responsibilities. • Delegate necessary authority to enable direct reports achieving their objectives. • Support direct reports in their work without taking direct ownership of their specific work.
Develop direct reports	• Set specific development objectives for direct reports. • Provide constructive and fact-based feedback. • Continuously include coaching as part of their leadership style.
Follow through on performance of direct reports	• Regularly initiate check-in conversations to support the direct reports in their work. • Frequently review work progress and performance of direct reports. • Respond in a timely manner to individual performance challenges and do not let performance challenges escalate.
Select team members	• Select qualified team members who contribute well to overall team performance. • Make the tough decisions and proactively replace team members who consistently fall short of delivering their objectives. • Select team members who hold potential to develop into other roles too.
Build the team	• Create an inclusive environment where teamwork and collaboration are valued. • Build a high level of engagement. • Create an open and trusting environment that encourages people to speak up.
Integrate upwards and sideways	• Keep the direct manager informed about progress. • In due course share anticipated obstacles. • Proactively coordinate work with relevant colleagues.

Figure 1.2. Leading Others: The Job to Be Done.
Source: Copyright Leadership Pipeline Institute.

don't confuse readers. The model should be used to help leaders focus on what is really important in their role.

The second column, **Required Activities**, makes the model hands-on and action oriented. This column answers questions such as "What do I do to set direction and empower and build the team?" Activities will differ from company to company; *some activities will change in the same company as the business progresses.* We expect all companies to base activities on their unique business needs. We are trying to give readers a starting point for thinking this through, not tell them what to do. We also expect leaders to phrase statements using their own language and terminology. Some organizations operate with "check-in" sessions, others operate with "one-on-one" sessions, though the purpose and content of the conversation is the same.

Figure 1.2 uses very simple language. We have seen again and again that using simple language to define what is expected leads to better understanding and more success. People go to work to do their best. But they often need to be shown what "best" looks like in a way that makes sense and in language they understand.

One of the key roles for leaders-of-leaders as we discuss in Chapter 4 is to develop leaders-of-others and assess their performance. The eternal challenge in completing assessments as described by leaders-of-leaders is that they are not always sure what to look for and how to make it fact based. If you define the leading-of-others role as in Figure 1.2, you not only support the leaders-of-others doing their leadership work but also you support the leaders-of-leaders doing their leadership work.

Finally, most businesses understand the importance of building a "leadership bank"—meaning creating leadership bench strength. You need to have confidence that all leaders are assessed on the same job to be done and that assessments are fact based. This very hands-on and job-to-be-done approach will also help focus on what's needed and minimize gender and cultural biases as well as unconscious biases, hence, support building a diverse organization.

In the chapters to come, we have illustrated what this can look like for some of the most common leadership roles across organizations.

Understanding the Transitions

Getting full value from the Leadership Pipeline requires a deep understanding of the transitions required as people move into a new leadership role. We want to make clear what these transitions involve. As we have discussed (and hopefully have made clear), stepping into a new leadership role demands a complete change in how the leader adds value. Some will be successful at making the transition one, two, or perhaps three times to new layers/roles. Others will struggle to make one, the transition to leading others. They all will need help.

Transitions are composed of three primary elements:

- Work values: what people believe is important and so becomes the focus of their effort and gets the highest priority

- Time application: the new job to be done requires time be allocated to these requirements and not to the old ones

- Skills: the capabilities required to execute new responsibilities

These three areas of transition constitute the **transition triad**. This triad gets more complicated as roles get bigger. The transition from one leadership layer/role to another does not happen unless these three things change appropriately. As we spell out, each passage requires that leaders acquire a new way of leading and leave the old ways behind.

Let's take a closer look at the transition triad by exploring a couple of fictional case studies.

Case study

Bob is at passage 1—leading others—having recently been promoted to be leader of his team. Previously, Bob had proven to be a crackerjack engineer, the best problem-solver in the department, and his superior technical skills earned him his promotion. As a leader, however, Bob relied on a hands-on, problem-solving approach that had worked for him as an individual contributor engineer over the past seven years. It is work that he enjoys and is comfortable doing; his work values dictate that he find the engineering solution himself. But it is also what prevents him from building and demonstrating leadership capability. Typically, Bob ends up competing with his own direct reports when a new assignment comes up. He keeps the hardest parts for himself because he believes he can do them better and faster. This leadership style suffocates the team and they end up just asking Bob for answers instead of fixing the challenges themselves. Though now in a leadership position, Bob still values technical work more than leadership work.

Case study

Maria, a former sales manager, is now the head of a business unit; she's at passage 4—from function leader to business leader. Over the course of her career Maria has aggressively pursued new customers and relishes the supplier-customer dynamic, spending a great deal of time in one-on-one customer interactions. She's been highly innovative with her service ideas and has consistently hit or exceeded sales targets for her group because of her approach. As the head of a business unit, Maria is encountering a number of new challenges.

She's finding it difficult to communicate with people in functions other than sales and hasn't been able to create a business model that her people can understand and relate to. She doesn't understand why engineering and manufacturing are always in disagreement and why deliveries are so late on new products. Frustrated by her inability to do what's required, Maria decides that she can "bull" her way through by relying on her strength. By focusing on deepening old and securing new customer relationships, she is back in her comfort zone. Unfortunately, that's only one of many things she needs to do in her current leadership position. This is the first time Maria has ever headed a multifunctional team, and she doesn't value the contributions of each function or understand their contribution to the success of the business. She has failed to become more strategic and less transactional. To be an effective business leader she needs strategic skills and she needs to value all functions.

Work Values

The phrase *work values* refers to the work you think is important and how you experience creating value on the job. Work values are, without doubt, the most important element in transitions and the most difficult to achieve. We can train people in skills and create schedules and systems that control where their time goes, but in reality, adjusting work values is more powerful when moving from one level to another.

The principle of work values being the most fundamental part of a transition is illustrated well in Bob's case. What makes a good day for Bob now is fixing a problem. What should be a good day for Bob is his team fixing problems based on how he has coached and developed them. In general, if work values are not adjusted, it is unlikely that any behavioral change will occur.

In Maria's case, her passion for customer activities, where she could bring her professionalism into play, was clearly evident. She didn't have the same enthusiasm when it came to integrating functions and taking a strategic approach to the business. It could easily be argued that she had not even fully transitioned into her function leadership role prior to becoming business leader. At this level it is not just about visiting customers and closing deals. She needs to value working with all functions on creating an even better customer value proposition as part of a business strategy.

Time Application

As leaders progress from one layer to another, they will find that the key to success is mostly about making other people successful.

Bob needs to set aside time for leadership work. It is not that he does not do any leadership work at all. When we looked at his calendar, we found that most check-in sessions with direct reports, performance reviews, and budget follow-ups were booked outside normal working hours. All the leadership work seems to come on top of the job instead of being the job. Bob knows that he is supposed to conduct quarterly structured performance reviews with each of his direct reports, so he might as well put them in the calendar 12 months ahead. Same with budget input. He knows it will take place in September. He might as well enter these events in his calendar early as a reminder.

Maria needs to spend time with all functions to get to know how they truly add value to the business and how each interacts with the other functions. She has to replace herself as sales manager with someone she trusts to run the function and let them do so. Unfortunately, what we often find is that newly appointed business leaders spend way too much time with the function they came from. This is the function that makes them feel comfortable and that they have enjoyed for many years. Initially they know much more about the function than their successor and hence they feel they create more value meeting with that function versus meeting with other functions. Business leaders will eventually run into significant challenges if they do not dedicate time to all functions. They can't build an effective business strategy until they understand how the functions create competitive advantage.

Skills

It is evident that each new leadership role requires new skills. Developing leaders' skills is usually the easiest of the three transition elements. It cannot be neglected just because it is evident.

In Bob's case, he needs to stop relying on his technical skills and learn to plan the work that needs to be done, select good people to do it, set objectives, hold people accountable for results, and offer feedback. This first turn is where he'll acquire people leadership and team leadership skills—skills that will be essential for him if he pursues future passages.

Maria clearly runs short of some key business leader skills: functional integration, execution, and creating a business system/ rhythm. Even though skills development is the easiest part of the transition, the skills needed at the function leader and business leader levels are not for everyone. As we previously suggested, Maria did not fully transition into the function leader role before becoming a business leader. It is too tough for most people in business leader roles to catch up on skills missing from previous roles while acquiring the new skills. This is unfortunately the reason we see many business leaders fail over time.

Interdependency

It is important to recognize that work values, time application, and skills are interdependent. You cannot master a transition by adjusting one and not the others. For instance, work values guide how you spend your time, because most people will tend to do first the things that are most important to them. Skills also guide how people spend their time. If you are good at stakeholder management, you tend to embrace that part of your job. People like doing what they are good at especially if they have previously earned recognition. Accordingly, a key to successful transitions lies in the dedication to become good at what is now required. This will support the shifting of work values. Leaders will start to appreciate what they need to do and find it easier to spend time doing it.

New Ways of Looking at Careers

As you become familiar with each leadership passage, you'll find yourself thinking about careers, development, promotions, and performance from a fresh perspective. What is more significant, this new perspective will provide you with the insights necessary to keep your leadership pipeline filled and flowing. Not only will it help you structure the right process to get the right leader in the right job on all levels, it will also enable you to ensure that they're working at the right levels and delivering appropriate value.

However, when you look at Figure 1.1 it is important to keep in mind that it is not a visualization of how to plan a career. Very few leaders enter the function and business leader roles; most leaders remain in leading-others roles. There are many ways of making a career—it's not just about moving to a bigger leadership role. It can be equally and for many people much more rewarding to stay in one type of leadership role and then make lateral career moves into other functions or geographies. Some leaders also skip leadership levels—even though it is not recommended. You may experience a leader-of-leaders who wasn't previously in a leader-of-others role. If they then move to a leader-of-others role, they still need to go through a transition. Likewise, you also see leaders-of-others or leaders-of-leaders moving into key specialist roles rather than continuously pursuing new leadership roles. A career these days can be a coat of many colors; having a good definition of requirements and accountability makes for a better discussion and plan.

If you keep the metaphor of a pipeline in mind, you can see how things might become clogged at the turns. Imagine a company where more than half the managers at each turn are operating with work values, time application, and skills that are not appropriate to their level; either they've skipped a level and never learned what they need to know or they're clinging to an old mode of leading that was successful for them in the past. In some companies, at least 50% of the people in leadership positions (usually at lower layers) are operating far below their assigned layer. They may have the potential to perform the job to be done, but that potential is going unfulfilled. In short, they're clogging up the system. Career planning for any organization can focus on proper placement.

Promoting people is a business decision. It is like any other investment decision. Applied the right way, the Leadership Portraits provide you with the facts you might require in any other business decision. It significantly increases the level of certainty in promotions.

As you reflect on the Leadership Portrait concept you will realize why operating with leadership competence models as the backbone of leadership assessment, leadership development, and succession planning is doomed to fail. Leadership competencies are input, but it is just one input out of three important ones. Also, the output part in terms of the job to be done is missing. Competency models have their merits, but not as a backbone system or an overall leadership framework.

The portraits play a key role in the development of leaders. Let's say you're asking yourself questions such as, "What is inhibiting this leader's performance?" "How can I help the leader perform even better?" Or, "Why has this leader not created development plans for their direct reports?" Most often the answer is that the leader lacks the right work values, has ineffective time management, or lacks skills. Accordingly, you need to design leadership development based on the entire transition triad and not just the skills.

When assessing whether a leader-of-others has potential to move into a leader-of-leaders role, determine if the leader in question has fully transitioned into their leading-others role. If they have, then you can compare the leading-of-others portrait with the leading-leaders portrait and ask yourself, "Has this leader-of-others demonstrated anything on the job that indicates they are ready to succeed as a leader-of-leaders?" "Have they demonstrated potential in relation to the required work values and skills?" In the absence of Leadership Portraits, you will most often find that discussions of leadership potential become very abstract.

Going Forward

No matter what type of organization you are in or your level of leadership responsibility, we trust you will find the information in the following chapters applicable in your environment. The Leadership Pipeline model is a very flexible model that organizations can adapt to their own situations and concerns. It's also a model designed with changing leadership accountabilities in mind. The traditional notions of what a leader needs to be and the extensive use of competence models are no longer the answer to the fundamental questions related to succession planning, leadership development, and performance management. The current business situation and other factors we have discussed previously are creating new requirements at all leadership levels and new types of leadership roles. We will address the broad variation of new leadership roles in Part III of this book.

To use the leadership pipeline approach effectively, you need to challenge traditional notions of leadership. Though you cannot hold leaders accountable for leadership unless you have a clear definition of the job to be done, you cannot develop leaders effectively unless you have an accurate development target. And you cannot have a meaningful discussion about leadership potential unless you base it on facts related to the relevant passage. Once you start developing leaders with this new reality in mind it will be that much easier to be successful on the human side of the business. In the following chapters, we will describe some of the most common leadership passages that the majority of leaders will experience one way or another.

Finally, we would like to warn you away from a mechanical implementation of the Leadership Pipeline concept. Each organization has to capture their company culture, unique organization structure, and business model. At the same time, you need to stay agile and ready to adjust. In other words, avoid three-ring binders and the paper exercise mentality that comes with them.

2

Leadership Pipeline Value Proposition

When it comes to trying a new model, an important question is whether implementation is worth it. There are always learning curves to climb and naysayers to convince. There are usually other initiatives competing for time and money.

Imagine a company that has a chief financial officer but doesn't have a general ledger, or a budget process, or a cost accounting system, or a capital allocation process that are tied together. That finance officer wouldn't have much success. Finance's architecture enables the entire organization to work with and talk about financial matters in a consistent way. Companies need an enduring architecture to focus leadership processes and programs. The architecture should set common standards for performance and for potential, differentiated by layer and roles of leadership. It should also establish language and processes to address issues, identify problems, and exploit opportunities effectively, as well as data for making decisions about everything from job transitions to performance improvement.

We trust you will see that applying the Leadership Pipeline architecture is more than worth it. When the architecture is adapted to your organization's specific situation, the benefits are certain, measurable, and visible to all. Common language is an undervalued benefit and a gift that keeps on giving. People cannot think about things for which they don't have language.

Strengthening Your Weakest Link

Every leader counts. Business is composed of many interconnected elements that must work together. Leaders make the connections happen so work can flow efficiently. They make sure the work gets done.

Given how dry the leadership pipeline is in many companies, the most common organizational response to this situation is surprising: adopting a "best and brightest" strategy. Organization after organization has decided that it can solve its leadership problem by finding and nurturing the top talent. Hiring gifted people makes sense as a tactic but not a strategy. Certainly, if there's an enormously talented individual whom you can recruit for your organization, you should do so. Strategically, however, this approach falls apart because of the scarcity of highly talented individuals. Not only will you have to pay through the nose for these people but also, what is more important, they will probably never develop fully. Some stars of the business world change jobs or companies so frequently that they have difficulty finishing what they started. They don't stay in one place long enough to learn from mistakes, master the right skills, or gain the experience needed for sustainable performance.

Although star performers can contribute a great deal to any company, there are not enough to go around. Today's companies need effective leaders at every level and in every location. Because of the information technology revolution, globalization, and other factors, leadership is a requirement up and down the line. To deliver on increasingly ambitious promises to customers, shareholders, employees, and other stakeholders, businesses need more fully performing leaders than ever before. This means finding a method that ensures more leaders will be prepared for and placed at the right leadership levels.

A recent idea emanating from economic analysis—weakest link versus strongest link investment decisions—is relevant here.

Which part of a team should be the focus of investment—the weakest link or the strongest link? The answer depends on how winning happens. For clarity, consider team sports where contribution to success and winning are visible. In basketball winning requires a lot of scoring. Having one or two or three great players out of 15 team members is enough to win a championship. Getting a player or two who can take the ball at one end of the court and move it all the way to the other end and score by themselves is a winning strategy. Two or three players who can score on their own, no matter how the opposition defends, is a necessary condition for success. In soccer, by contrast, there are very few scores. It routinely takes seven or eight or more passes to score one goal. Many games are won with one or two goals. Everyone in the passing chain has to perform effectively to enable that shot on goal. Certainly having a few good at scoring goals is necessary but they won't get a chance if the passing breaks down. In basketball investing heavily in superstars works. In soccer investing in everyone to be sure they all can catch and pass at a high level is required.

Business is usually more like soccer than basketball. All leaders have to perform effectively, and successful businesses invest in all of them. The Leadership Pipeline tells you what skills are required for all leaders, how they should spend their time, and what work they should consider important. It also provides differentiation by layer so the right development can be provided. Start-ups and very small businesses might do better investing in the strongest link—for example, skewing investment toward making the design leader or the sales leader great. That strategy should be changed as soon as the business starts to grow.

Reducing Your Soft Costs

An important but underused business idea is the notion of "soft costs." Every dollar spent by a business that doesn't directly tie to design, production, sale, and delivery of the product can be considered a soft cost. Some soft costs are quite necessary, such as recruiting talent, keeping the books, and helping the community. But most soft costs are destructive to the business, such as down time, including waiting for instructions; rework for fixing mistakes; and employee turnover.

We believe the most destructive soft cost is salary paid to leaders who work at the wrong level—in other words, they are paid more than are their direct reports, often considerably more, but they do the same work as their direct reports.

Leadership productivity isn't discussed very often but it should be. And though it's hard to measure in absolute terms, it can be considered in relative terms. You can ask yourself if your business is operating more effectively this year compared to last. If so, and if you can ascribe the improvement to leadership actions, then leadership productivity is improving. A more concrete measure is reducing the number of leaders working on the wrong things or working at the wrong level. That means they're assigned to one level but are working at another, usually lower, level. That scenario impedes the contribution of those above and below. In addition, salary dollars are wasted, important work isn't getting done, productivity is damaged, and morale is lowered.

Universal Bank of Leaders Required

Underlying our focus on the Leadership Pipeline is the need every company has for people who can and will do leadership work at increasingly higher levels. Call it *a bank of leaders*. Successful companies grow, so they add people to do the increasing volume of work. Someone has to select them, define meaningful roles, establish goals, train and develop them, plan their work, give feedback, and reward them. The more growth there is the more leaders are needed at lower and higher levels. Having those leaders ready to assume new or increased leadership roles is an important challenge for all organizations, not just start-ups or high tech. The Leadership

Pipeline principles and practices provides a roadmap for that development.

Leadership failure is everywhere. Employee unrest and constant movement can be traced directly to poor leadership, particularly at lower levels. This is fixable. Planning for future talent needs, developing people rather than hoping the right person walks in the door, and learning to win with the people you have are necessary leadership contributions. Most of it is very teachable.

The fewer leaders you have who are ineffective at leadership, the more leadership development is needed. Having a bank of leaders is more valuable than a bank of money. Through our own hands-on work, the Leadership Pipeline has proven to be an effective roadmap in every industry, country, organization size, and state of business. The variables that determine how well it works are valuing leadership work and holding leaders accountable for it.

Building a bank of talent requires an approach different from what we most often experience. We clearly see an increased investment in top management and we are sure many business schools can echo this observation. Many organizations also have a structured approach to basic onboarding of new leaders. But most training is competency or skills based—not truly helping leaders in the full transition in work values and time application. In addition, many programs are not interlinked from bottom to top, and there are almost no programs dealing with the key transition into the leading leaders role.

In large organizations it seems to be common sense to leave all frontline training to the different business units or geographical units, whereas senior talent programs and executive development are designed at enterprise level. "We are a decentralized organization" we often hear. The consequence is that you will never be able to get the broad-based talent flow to happen. Looking back at our analogy with the finance function previously in this chapter: Can you imagine a CFO saying that they can only measure revenue and profit on the key customers managed by the global sales function? So, they know nothing about 80% of the company's revenue and profit? Of course we can't envision that. You expect the global finance department to install systems and processes that secure full financial transparency and a common approach to manage money across the entire business. If you truly subscribe to the idea that "our people are our greatest asset," then you need the same approach to the people processes as you have for financial processes.

Based on the success many companies have experienced, no matter what they do or where they operate, we believe we have captured first principles for leadership development success. Therefore, they can't be ignored. First principles are timeless, as ours are proving to be. A new generation of leaders has discovered the Leadership Pipeline and they comment on it now from all over the world on LinkedIn.

The strength of your leadership is a true barometer of future business success. It is well worth the effort to understand and apply these principles.

A Model for Past, Present, and Future

In recent years, organizations have become increasingly aware of the need to build sustainable enterprises, not just ones that create short-term profits. We've heard from organizations that the Leadership Pipeline model helps them focus on the future development of leaders rather than just present performance issues.

In most cases we have seen, standards for making judgments about people are different for different activities. Performance ratings, promotions, bonuses, and participation in development are based on varying standards, causing confusion for those trying to make judgments as well as for those being judged.

When we wrote The Leadership Pipeline, we knew a need existed for a central architecture, a framework shared by all leaders to ensure consistency of judgment and application on the human side of the business so that a cumulative leadership effect is achieved. What we've learned in the interim is that this need is far more compelling and widespread than we initially assumed.

What we have also learned is how the Leadership Pipeline model, to an increasing extent, serves a broader business purpose and is linked to many agendas other than leadership development and succession planning. Next we share four cases.

Case 1: Internationalization of the Business/Significant Change

For 20 years, a company had grown very big in one country with small and mid-sized subsidiaries in about 15 other countries. Their workforce distribution was 70% employees in the country of origin and 30% in other countries. Seven years from now they expect these two numbers to be reversed.

Their existing leadership framework, talent approach, and people agenda had been significantly culturally biased toward their country of origin and focus had by far been on developing leaders in that country for the top 100 positions. It was assessed that this approach stood in the way of international expansion. They needed to fundamentally transform their leadership and talent approach.

Case 2: Significant Improvement of the Gender Diversity of the Leadership Population

The company had assessed that it was critical to the business to significantly increase the ratio of female leaders from middle managers and upwards. They analyzed the reasons why women did not pursue or were not selected for managerial roles.

Some of the most striking reasons were as follows:

- Leaders selecting other leaders did not have any tools to help them be objective in their selection processes. The result was that the dominating male population often assessed leadership qualities seen from a male perspective rather than from an objective perspective.

- It was unclear for applicants for leadership roles what was really required to be a leader at that company. The result was that many female applicants had an inaccurate understanding of what was required and therefore refrained from pursuing leadership roles.

• The people review process in which performance and potential were assessed was flawed, because the assessments were generally far from fact-based.

Multiple other reasons were identified, but these reasons were clogging their pipeline of leaders.

In both case 1 and case 2, the key to success was to apply the Leadership Pipeline model, which is culturally neutral and focused on the job that needs to be done, rather than the personal traits or competencies from a particular culture or gender. Further, they needed to develop transition criteria that could help assess a person's potential to transition into or up to leadership positions.

Case 3: Redesign and Improve Efficiency in the Project Versus Line Organization

A large, asset building, project organization needed to significantly increase their scalability. Accordingly, they reorganized the distribution of power in the organization. Going forward, the asset projects would operate much like a business unit with support from the line functions. A separate organization overseeing likely engineering and construction for future projects was also put in place.

The scalability was achieved by designing a highly matrixed organization with 85% of all staff members consistently working in a matrix setup. This enabled the organization to better stretch the delivery capability while ensuring that they looked forward not only for tomorrow but also three to five years ahead in both technical and competence development.

Their projects were typically three-plus-years long. Up to half of the project staff members would spend 90% of their time in the project during those three years. The fundamental challenge for the organization was effective people selection, deselection, development, and assessment in this organizational structure.

As such, the core leadership roles were split between the project organization and the function organization. Furthermore, in principle, all project team members had two leaders—their project leader and their function leader, so it seemed they were well covered for leadership. The reality, however, was the project members felt they had no leader at all because so many things fell between the chairs.

The key to success was using the Leadership Pipeline model because this enabled development of an integrated leadership framework for project managers and function managers. This way, they obtained full transparency of how the leadership work was distributed between the project managers and the function managers.

Case 4: Speed Up the Execution of the Business Strategy

The organization had engaged in a delayering project facilitated by a strategy consulting company. The aim was to improve their ability to execute by removing two layers of leadership and increasing the average number of direct reports to seven. This initiative required a reorganization of the existing structure and rethinking the business flow. One of the core solutions recommended by the strategy consultants was to increase the typical span of control. Span of control matters as any leader can attest. So why do we end up in a situation where too many leaders have too few direct reports?

There can be many reasons for this. We have learned over time that many leaders avoid having more than four or five direct reports because every extra direct report requires that they spend more time on leadership. This limits the time they can spend on "doing work themselves." This attitude is enabled by the lack of an effective transition into leadership roles. They still find more comfort and satisfaction in doing work themselves and solving day-to-day problems rather than doing leadership work.

Of course, in a transformation project you can just redesign the organization by force and secure the desired number of layers and span of control. However, if you don't address the leadership challenges at the same time, three or four years later you will be back where you started. Your leaders will easily find ways to decrease their span of control over time, if that is what they want.

The key to success was redesigning their leadership development programs to embrace the full transition in work values, time application, and skills. A fundamental adjustment to leaders' work values—meaning how they truly experience adding value and what they like doing—is critical for leaders to enjoy having an appropriate number of direct reports.

How to Build Needed Architecture

More so now than ever before, the architecture described in *The Leadership Pipeline* must be understood and used by leaders at all levels—not only those who lead the human resources (HR) department. Understanding and using the architecture will make leaders more effective, especially if they are a leader-of-leaders. HR people have a critical role to play, but it is an architecture and engineering role, not an owner/operator role. Leaders are the operators; they make the judgments, and they will live with the successes or failures of those judgments. HR is the engineering function accountable for design, usability, value, and quality of the architecture.

Our global society can't continue to withstand the enormous failure rates of those in leadership positions combined with the deepening shortage of capable people willing to lead our businesses. The challenge must be addressed in ways that are significantly more systematic, so the growth of leaders becomes organic and predictably successful. Given the growing need for more effective leadership development models and the emerging obstacles to such development, this book is even more relevant and needed today than it was 10 years ago. Our readers have told us that *The Leadership Pipeline* has changed the way their companies approach the human side of business at a fundamental level.

PART II

FIVE LEADERSHIP
PIPELINE PASSAGES

3

Leading Others

Absolutely nothing is more valuable to an individual con-tributor at work than having a good leader. The leader makes the work experience more pleasant, facilitates the completion of tasks without undue stress, answers questions, and contributes to the development of their employees. An ineffective leader, however, makes the work experience unpleasant, increases stress, and leaves people scratching their heads and looking elsewhere.

From an enterprise perspective, more than 80% of all employ-ees report to a leader-of-others, so leaders-of-others have the most direct impact of all leaders on reactions such as morale, motiva-tion, attitude, job satisfaction, quality, and employee retention.

Different leaders-of-others may have different leadership styles, work in different business/organizational contexts, or operate in different cultures, but the core value equation for leaders-of-others is still the same: they create value through others. Let us explore that further.

If an individual contributor improves their total output by 10%, they are the only ones to make the difference. If we exclude exter-nal factors, an individual contributor can essentially increase only their "output" by working harder or smarter.

This value equation changes dramatically when moving into a leader-of-others role. If a leader-of-others is tasked with improving output by 10%, the entire team must be involved and not just the leader. Consequently, a leader-of-others cannot improve the output of their team just by producing more themselves. They need their team to produce more.

The most effective way for a leader-of-others to improve the overall team result is by enabling the individual contributors to improve their results. This is done through leadership work, including selecting the right team members, building a strong team, coaching and developing the individual contributors, setting direction, building purpose, empowering direct reports, following up on performance, and continuously prioritizing tasks.

Intellectually, this is easy to appreciate for all leaders-of-others. Yet, in our experience, many frontline leaders struggle in their roles. The individual contributors pay an immediate price for this; the organization pays the ultimate price.

The Job to Be Done

In Figure 3.1, we have summarized the fundamental job to be done by a leader-of-others. Later in this chapter, we discuss how the role of leader-of-others can differ based on industry, organizational structure, and business model. What we are outlining is the job to be done in most leader-of-others roles. However, it is not a job description, and must be customized for use in any organization.

To elaborate on each category of work in turn: leaders-of-others plan and set direction to build purpose for the team.

Leaders-of-Others Set the Direction for Their Team

This includes defining roles, setting business objectives and deliverables for each team member, and ensuring they understand how their business objectives tie into the overall team objectives and overall company goals. In everyday life, they guide team members on how to prioritize their work—and when their people understand the business better, they can be engaged to help define the business objectives.

The Work	Required Activities
Set direction	• Clearly define the roles and priorities of direct reports. • Create a clear understanding of how direct reports' personal business objectives tie into overall team and business-unit objectives. • Engage direct reports in establishing personal business objectives.
Empower	• Enable direct reports to deal effectively with their responsibilities. • Delegate necessary authority to enable direct reports achieving their objectives. • Support direct reports in their work without taking direct ownership of their specific work.
Develop direct reports	• Set specific development objectives for direct reports. • Provide constructive and fact-based feedback. • Continuously include coaching as part of their leadership style.
Follow through on performance of direct reports	• Regularly initiate check-in conversations to support the direct reports in their work. • Frequently review work progress and performance of direct reports. • Respond in a timely manner to individual performance challenges and do not let performance challenges escalate.
Select team members	• Select qualified team members who contribute well to overall team performance. • Make the tough decisions and proactively replace team members who consistently fall short of delivering their objectives. • Select team members who hold potential to develop into other roles too.
Build the team	• Create an inclusive environment where teamwork and collaboration are valued. • Build a high level of engagement. • Create an open and trusting environment that encourages people to speak up.
Integrate upwards and sideways	• Keep the direct manager informed about progress. • In due course share anticipated obstacles. • Proactively coordinate work with relevant colleagues.

Figure 3.1. Leading Others: The Job to Be Done.
Source: Copyright Leadership Pipeline Institute.

Not getting this right is one of the most common reasons why a new leader's employees leave within the first 12 months. We have heard the same story many times in many variations: "After six months in the job, I am still not sure how I personally make a difference . . . . I like my colleagues and the company, but I need to find a job where I understand what to deliver and that what I am being held accountable for is meaningful."

Leaders-of-Others Empower the Team

Empowering includes delegating tasks *and* sufficient decision-making authority to get things done efficiently. The leader still supports the team, but the important balance is to support them in their work without taking direct ownership of any of their specific work. This also means taking a structured approach to engaging direct reports through check-in conversations when they discuss how work is progressing and offering their guidance and expertise.

Delegating presents a formidable challenge to novice leaders. It's one thing to figure out what needs to be done and who needs to do it; it's quite another, and much more psychologically difficult, to let go of work that they were trained to do and that has helped them become successful. This is a very difficult step for first-time leaders to take, and they're usually able to take it only when they realize that delegation is not abdication and produces better results.

Leaders-of-Others Develop Their Direct Reports

This responsibility is a key performance success factor. Performance as a leader-of-others equals the consolidated performance of the team. The best way to ensure team performance is by knowing where the work stands and coaching direct reports on how to solve any problems they are having. The better they get, the better the leader's performance. This is not just about sending people on training programs. On the contrary, this is about knowing what is getting done and what isn't and then coaching on the spot. In our experience, this real-time coaching and on-the-job development is the most powerful development option. It avoids hold-ups in results and makes employees better at their jobs immediately in many cases.

In Figure 4.3 (in the next chapter) you'll see that most leaders-of-others know they need to spend more time on developing their direct reports but seem unable to find the time to do it. It is likely that they are not taking a structured approach to developing their people. Something such as a simple development plan where they define development objectives and list actions to be taken are most often not in place. Actions that will remedy shortcomings and/or add new skills to obtain better results are in everyone's best interest. Concise and focused actions work much better than generalizations. This is how leaders-of-others truly add value.

Leaders-of-Others Follow Through on the Performance of Their Direct Reports

This responsibility is much more than just conducting an annual or semiannual performance review. It includes frequent check-in sessions when work progress and performance are discussed and time is spent on coaching and guiding direct reports.

When making performance assessments, leaders-of-others must ensure that they are thorough and fact-based. In particular, when assessing people's behavior, they must pay attention to their biases. People are different and they achieve great results in different ways that may not be the conventional way. Those doing the work can often find better ways.

When things are not going well, they should be addressed in a timely manner. Letting performance challenges stagnate is neither good for the leader nor the direct report. We can't count the number of times when we have facilitated people reviews and the following situation appears. A leader-of-others describes one of their direct reports as a low performer. The facts clearly indicate low performance. When we ask the leader, "How did your direct report react when they were made aware the first time and second time that they were not performing at the right level?" It almost hurts to share here that one of the common responses is "Well, I have not really had that conversation yet." Most "difficult" conversations are only difficult because they are long overdue.

Performance assessment should go hand-in-hand with a development plan. Likely actions that will remedy shortcomings and/or add new skills to obtain better results are in everyone's best interest. Concise and focused actions work better than generalizations.

Leaders-of-Others Select Their Team Members

This responsibility is the most significant decision most leaders make, in our experience. All leaders must learn to hire the right people to do the required tasks. Though many of them quickly learn how to hire people with the talent and experience to do a given job properly, many find it more difficult to hire people who "fit" a company's values and practices. In most cases when people are asked to leave an organization after only a few months, it's because the individual doesn't fit the culture. Although some people depart because they lack the talent for a specific job, most simply lack the beliefs, values, and ability to conform to an established style of working. Becoming astute about hiring people who are well matched to the work style and beliefs of the organization can greatly enhance a first-time leader's effectiveness. Investing the necessary time to identify qualified team candidates who will contribute to the overall team performance deserves the highest priority.

The other side of selecting is deselecting. Leaders need to be willing to take the tough path and proactively replace team members who consistently fall short of delivering on their objectives. We have so often heard a conversation in which a leader states, "Yes, but it was fine they left; they were not really performing anyway." What is this all about? If they were "not really performing," then why didn't the leader take charge of the situation and replace that person? And note, "taking charge" doesn't only mean "letting go" of the person; it could also mean increasing focus to support the person in getting to the right performance level. A leader needs to be aware that someone is not performing, because the entire team probably knows it, too. They often know it before the leader does. By not acting on the situation, the leader is telling their team that poor performance is okay.

Leaders-of-Others Build Their Team

With their team members in place, leaders need to build the team. Strong teamwork is a powerful method for strengthening performance. Having good colleagues is also a major retention factor for people. Leaders must create an environment in which teamwork and cooperation are valued. They need a team in which people learn from each other and are open about mistakes and how they need to develop. Peer learning is powerful, but it requires an open and trusting environment in which the team feels psychologically safe. Psychological safety here is understood as the team members feeling confident they can show weaknesses, express opinions, and question the status quo without fear of negative consequences. They simply feel accepted and respected for who they are.

Leaders-of-Others Integrate Upwards and Sideways

Effective leaders-of-others look beyond the team. They need to integrate upwards with the direct manager or manager in matrix organizations, as well as integrate sideways with immediate peers and for some also with colleagues in entirely different functions. Keeping their boss informed about work progress and potential obstacles makes it much easier for the boss to delegate authority. Today, many organizations work at breaking down the hierarchies and enabling decisions to be made at the frontline of the business. Digitization has made significant data and substantial information available to leaders-of-others. A prerequisite for this to be successful is that leaders-of-others proactively coordinate work, share priorities, and fix problems with their reports rather than escalating the problems. Work gets done faster that way, and digitization makes it possible.

The Transition to the Role

When people are appointed to their first leader-of-others position, they often feel they have made it. All their hard work as an individual contributor has finally been rewarded, and they see a leadership assignment as a cause for celebration. They call their partner, make reservations at a favorite restaurant, or buy themselves a gift.

In reality the hard work is just starting. To be successful as a first-time leader requires a major transition. Many people are not adequately prepared for it. Perhaps the most difficult aspect of this transition is that first-time leaders are responsible for getting work done through others rather than on their own. Although new leaders may recognize this transition intellectually, their activities might not change. Giving up the tasks and responsibilities that earned them the promotion is a tremendously difficult. It stands in the way of making the transition for many leaders-of-others.

Figure 3.2 offers an overview of the core difference in work values, time application, and skills between an individual contributor and a leader-of-others. The list represents what applies to most leader-of-others roles. In your organization, you may need to add to these depending on what else the specific roles require.

In Chapter 1 we described our action research done since 2010. In Figure 3.3 you see the consolidated results for leaders-of-others.

Leading Self
WORK VALUES
- Achieving results through personal proficiency
- Delivering high-quality technical or professional work
- Living company's values

TIME APPLICATION
- Daily discipline (arrival, departure)
- Meeting personal deadlines for projects by managing one's own time

SKILLS
- Technical or professional proficiency
- Team player
- Building relationships for personal results
- Using company tools, processes, and procedures

Leading Others
WORK VALUES
- Achieving results through others
- Success of direct reports and unit
- Self as leader

TIME APPLICATION
- Annual planning (budget, projects)
- Making time available for direct reports
- Managerial work

SKILLS
- Job design
- Selecting
- Delegating
- Coaching
- Giving feedback
- Performance management
- Communicating and climate setting
- Building the team
- Building psychological safety

Figure 3.2. Leading Self Versus Leading Others: Core Differences in Work Values, Time Application, and Skills.

Source: Drotter Human Resources, Inc., and Leadership Pipeline Institute.

What were the two or three main challenges you faced during the first three to six months after moving into your leader-of-others role?	What two or three things do you miss most about being an individual contributor?	What two or three things would you like to spend more time on in your current position, but seem unable to find time for?	What are the two or three most important skills you have come to realize you need as a leader-of-others?
1. Letting go of individual contributor work 2. Delegating 3. Setting objectives 4. Leading former colleagues 5. Prioritizing for team	1. Being on top of everything 2. Having time for myself 3. Getting more frequent recognition from direct manager 4. Independence 5. Feeling the satisfaction of delivering results myself	1. Coaching and developing direct reports 2. Building the team 3. "Me time" 4. "Face time" 1&1s, rather than just online 5. My own development	1. Delegating 2. Motivating 3. Coaching 4. Leading remote team members 5. People-managing tools

Figure 3.3. Consolidated Results for Leaders-of-Others.
Source: Copyright Leadership Pipeline Institute.

Work Values

The most difficult change when moving from leading self to leading others is the need to start valuing obtaining results through others. It starts by developing a *leadership mindset*. That means starting each day by asking, "How is my team doing and what can I do to improve their performance?"

Case study

Emma had been a recruiter within the HR function in a large logistics company for three years. On average, she would interview four or five people a day. One day, her leader, Evelyn, asked Emma if she would be interested in replacing her and taking on the team leader role. Emma had never thought about herself in the team leader role, but she asked Evelyn what to expect in that role compared to her current role.

(continued)

"Well, if you say yes to the position, you should be aware that your everyday work will change somewhat. For the past few years, you have been finding and testing applicants, conducting interviews, writing candidate reports, and discussing candidates with the different business managers. In the role of team leader, for a team of eight people, you would still conduct a few interviews, but the rest of the time would be spent on coaching your team on their work, just as I have done with you. You would be responsible for ensuring that all recruiters use our recruitment tools and processes correctly. Most important, you are currently measured on your personal results. As the team leader, you will be measured on the consolidated results of all team members."

"It all sounds good and exciting, but I should probably think it through and consider the pros and cons," Emma replied. "Can I let you know in a few days?"

On the way home, Emma's mind was spinning. The job as a leader-of-others would significantly increase her status—not to mention her paycheck. She could easily envisage sharing this news with friends and family. However, in her current role, Emma experienced people coming to her with questions because she understood how to interpret the psychometric tools much better than her colleagues, and she actually found it a bit tiring when colleagues asked for her advice on various topics. Of course, it's nice to be asked and to feel appreciated, but she felt that it was taking her away from her own work. She couldn't help thinking that if she were to conduct fewer interviews with applicants, she couldn't be sure that the right people were being matched to the right jobs. There was also the matter of losing control of her own performance. She would now have to achieve results through others. Two days later, Emma said no to the job.

This is one of the more fortunate cases. Emma said no in time. She wasn't motivated by creating results through others. The feeling that "I can't get my job done if I have too many direct reports" makes leadership seem like a trap, and Emma avoided that trap by being realistic about what she really values in her job.

Other people may not be that clear about what they value and what they do not value. They will say yes to the job and then either discover that they do value it or maybe develop into valuing it. Valuing getting results through others remains the most difficult part of being in a leader-of-others role.

Time Application

In our discussions with leaders-of-others about where their time goes, most conclude that they should spend more time on leadership work and give it higher priority.

How much time should they spend on leadership work? The most important factor is how many direct reports they have. If they have five direct reports, they may perform very well as leaders by spending about one third of their time on leading, whereas 30 direct reports can make their leadership work almost full time. Another factor is the necessary frequency of one-to-one conversations, which must be given sufficient time to complete. It can be substantial in knowledge work and research.

Consequently, the amount of time required for leadership work is an individual matter. The important part is that you take a close look at Figure 3.1 outlining the leadership work required of leaders-of-others and then do your own calculation. What is important, however, besides structured leadership work, is to make time available for your direct reports at their request. Making yourself available during the day avoids the trap of feeling that you are being disturbed whenever they approach you.

One way to test if enough time is being spent on leadership work is knowing with certainty that all team members know what to do, are doing it correctly, feel they are learning, and feel they have a good future in this company.

Skills

If you examine the required skills for a leader-of-others, you may conclude they are not technically that difficult to acquire. After all, most companies have performance management tools that are easy to use. You can find many simple feedback and coaching models. Even though a large portion of the leaders-of-others whom we meet have already attended some sort of first-line leader training, they still struggle.

The reality is that it is easy to learn a given feedback model, but that is just the technical part. The real value-adding part is taking a structured, fact-based approach and applying it consistently. A lack of facts is what keeps many leaders from giving feedback.

A new leader can easily learn one of the coaching models. However, these models work best when they sit down for a quiet moment to talk to their direct reports. That is not the everyday situation for many leaders. Leaders need to develop a *coaching leadership style* in which they turn a team meeting, a question at the coffee machine, a performance conversation, or a project meeting into a coaching situation.

Another example is job design. Job design is rarely the focus of training for leaders-of-others. Perhaps it's because people consider them inherent skills or ones that are easily acquired. It may be that organizations assume there are natural dividing lines for work—geography for salespeople or process steps for manufacturing people—and that job assignments flow from these natural divisions. Though it's true that some existing parameters make it easier to assign tasks, there is also a need for judgment—especially when first-line employees feel tremendously overworked and cut off from their bosses. Downsizing, delayering, merging companies, and other factors have made employees feel as though they have too much to do, aren't appreciated for what they do, and have no one to talk to about their situation. First-line leaders who know how to design a job effectively can avoid employees' negative feelings and make them feel the assignment is important; they can give employees a sense that they're developing highly marketable skills that will enhance their career prospects.

Accordingly, acquiring the right skills in this role requires much more than exposure to various tools and techniques. Practice and feedback are needed to develop most skills.

Typical Transition Issues

For most people, moving from an individual contributor role to a leader-of-others role is not without its challenges. Let's review the typical pitfalls using some examples. (See Figure 3.4.)

Typical Transition Issues

- Finding more satisfaction in one's own contribution than in team members' contributions
- Micromanaging instead of delegating
- Competing with direct reports about "knowing best"
- Avoiding tough conversations with direct reports
- Considering questions from direct reports a disturbance rather than opportunities to coach and develop them

Figure 3.4. Typical Transition Issues for Leaders-of-Others.
Source: Copyright Leadership Pipeline Institute.

Finding More Satisfaction in One's Own Contribution Than in Team Members' Contributions

Case study

When Zhang became a regional sales manager for a large pharmaceutical company, he saw it as an opportunity to earn more money and have more influence within the organization.

(continued)

When the position was offered, he didn't hesitate even though he loved his previous job as a salesperson. He'd enjoyed the autonomy given him, largely working out of his home, traveling the region, and meeting a variety of physicians and hospital administrators.

As a sales manager with eight sales representatives reporting to him, Zhang has had to spend much of his time in the field observing his reps, hiring, and training new people, going to meetings with other sales managers, and doing a great deal of paperwork (assessments, reports, and the like). Not only was he upset that his autonomy had been taken away but also he was frustrated by all the paperwork. The psychological satisfaction of closing a sale evaporated when he became a sales manager.

It's possible that Zhang might have made this first leadership passage successfully if he had been given the coaching to understand the required transition. It would have given him a better understanding of what was expected of him. Though it's possible that Zhang wasn't cut out to be a leader, it's also possible that he could have adjusted to that role if someone had coached him and helped him to reconfigure his work values.

Zhang's company did not have a set of leadership expectations. Nor had they outlined the required work values, time application, and skills required to be successful as a leader-of-others. You could argue that Zhang's manager, Aaliyah, selected Zhang for the role blindfolded because she did not have the core criteria in place to assess Zhang's readiness for the role. Likewise, Zhang may have accepted the role blindfolded. His primary motivation was more money and more influence. He should have thought, "Great, I always wanted to lead a team and create results through others." Had someone shown him an overview of the job that needed to be done and the required work values and time application, he might have taken himself off the leadership track before it even started.

A full transition in this work value comes when you get at least the same satisfaction from the success of your employees as you do from your own success.

Micromanaging Instead of Delegating

Case study

Aimee used to lead a team of seven people. They were all located in the same building sitting at two adjacent four-person tables in an open office environment. She was spoken of as "a solid leader." Good results from the team, engagement scores meeting company targets, willing to promote her own people for other internal jobs, and so forth. During COVID, all employees were sent home because being present was not critical for their roles. Only three months later, Aimee went down with stress-related symptoms.

Aimee's manager, Jamal, had a number of individual conversations with Aimee and her team members and concluded that the stress was clearly work-related. Jamal learned that Aimee had managed her people very closely. She had not set up broader business objectives for her team; she delegated specific tasks. Each team member had more than one task, but they reported back to Aimee whenever any task was completed. Also, Aimee would, on a daily basis, follow up on a specific task whenever the task crossed her mind.

Leading people remotely made Aimee's leadership style ineffective. Aimee went down with stress and was removed as leader. Today, the company has introduced a hybrid work environment where people can work up to three days from home per week. Jamal assessed that under these circumstances Aimee wouldn't be successful in the role. He could not convince her of the need to relinquish micromanaging.

There is an interesting extra angle to this case. We came across it in a company where we implemented the Leadership Pipeline concept. When we met Jamal he asked us if we had a training program on remote leadership. When we began to understand the case with Aimee, we told Jamal that this is not about remote leadership. It was the remote leadership situation that revealed the problem. The problem is the lack of core transition into the role. Aimee does not value creating results through others. She values doing things herself with practical help from seven people! The reality is that many frontline leaders can compensate for their failure to transition as long as they sit right next to their team. Their priority is not to make the transition but rather to deliver the required results. In a hybrid or remote leadership role, it all falls apart. This is also worth remembering when we assess leadership performance and potential for leaders-of-others. The results may be there, but are we sure they are leading, not just controlling?

Competing with Direct Reports About "Knowing Best"

Many leaders-of-others are promoted to their first leader-of-others role because they are the most knowledgeable and professionally skilled member of their team. Accordingly, they often do "know best" or at the very least, they are always able to add a little something, identify flaws, and adjust structure or language in whatever solution or proposal their direct reports produce.

Case study

Elijah had been team leader for nine people in a legal department for about 18 months. It is a large international medical devices company, and his team was responsible for ensuring patents protect their intellectual property. Besides leading the team, Elijah was also considered the absolute key specialist within this professional area. Over the past three months, Elijah had been discussing with his manager, Alison, that he felt too many of his team members were not really stepping up in the role even though they had the skills to do so, and they were getting consistent feedback and coaching. Alison was a skilled leader-of-leaders. So, she asked if she could sit in on a couple of Elijah's team meetings and if she and Elijah could discuss a couple of specific work cases before Elijah gave individual feedback on them. Alison observed at the team meeting that whatever was discussed, Elijah would be the one closing the discussion by "trumping" with some additional perspectives, insight, or personal experience. She observed the same thing when she discussed the work cases with Elijah. Based on this, Alison chatted with Elijah about how he might be paralyzing his direct reports. They knew that whatever work they did, Elijah would know best, and he would make minor, unnecessary adjustments to any work they did. Elijah's first response to Alison was that he just wanted to train and develop his direct reports. Alison pointed out, they were not developing, which was the reason why she and Elijah were having this conversation in the first place. Discussing it further, Elijah realized that he felt the only way he could justify being the leader of the team was by "knowing best" and, accordingly, he never missed a chance to demonstrate it.

The point is not that a leader-of-others shouldn't contribute to correcting errors or contribute to solutions. The point is that the leader should to do it for the right reasons. Sometimes they simply need to let go even if they could add a little value. Otherwise, the team gets used to the leader fixing things and they give up trying to do complete work. Also, the leader should require team members to take end-to-end responsibility for their work. Otherwise, they will never learn from their successes and failures.

Avoiding Tough Conversations with Direct Reports

Tough conversations are, by their very nature, difficult, and thus not something most people want to do. In our emerging leader programs, we usually ask what they most look forward to about becoming a leader-of-others and what they least look forward to. Tough conversations always rank at the top of the "least look forward to" category. Most companies include something in their leadership expectations about "proactively dealing with performance issues," "not shying away from difficult conversations," "not letting performance issues escalate," and so on. All organizations seem to experience this challenge.

The challenge can be increased when first-time leaders are promoted from within their team. A conversation that is already tough has to be conducted with a former peer. Nevertheless, it is part of the job that needs to get done. The trick is to figure out why you, the leader, ended up in this situation in the first place.

You have set clear business objectives, you have given consistently fact-based feedback, you have established a development plan and provided ongoing coaching, and yet one of your employees is not performing. You have done everything in your power to set up your employee for success—and yet they do not perform. How tough is that conversation, really? It is not a preferred or nice conversation, but is it tough or, in actuality, is it fairly straightforward?

In our experience, the reason many conversations are tough is because we have not taken the time to do our leadership work. Their business objectives are a bit unclear; we sense the person is not performing, but we lack facts, we have not really taken a structured approach to support the person developing into the job, and so on. Now the same conversation becomes tough and can easily turn into an endless back-and-forth discussion.

So, the best way to handle tough conversations is not by avoiding them. It is setting clear expectations, providing ongoing feedback and coaching, and having frequent fact-based performance conversations. It should fit into a basic manager/employee dialogue schedule.

Considering Questions from Direct Reports a Disturbance Rather Than Opportunities to Coach and Develop Them

Perhaps the simplest skill—and the one that many new leaders never had to consider as individual contributors—is just being available. This doesn't mean just keeping the office door open and grudgingly answering questions. It's much more of an attitude than an event. People sense when leaders are approachable. Everything from their speech to their body language communicates accessibility (or the lack of it). This is really much more of a work values and time application issue than a skill set. When leaders believe that being approachable is crucial to their leadership role, they make themselves available, both physically and emotionally.

It is, of course, flattering to be needed by other people. Unfortunately, it is easy to develop the feeling that people coming to you during the working day are an interruption of their own individual contributor work. Leaders may easily develop the feeling that they are lagging behind with their own work while they are in the process of helping their employees.

When progressing from being an individual contributor to a leader-of-others, it is necessary to adjust work values to include the fact that they are no longer responsible for only what they actually produce. People depend on them—and they depend on their people getting their job done. Essentially, leaders need to look at every conversation as a part of the job, as an opportunity to develop their people by helping them improve their performance. Setting their reports up for success is good for the leader, for them, and for the whole organization.

Variations of the Role

Many leadership roles are not pure leadership. Leaders spend some portion of their time on individual contributor work. Some have three or four direct reports—they easily spend 80% of their time on individual contributor work. Others have 20 or 30 direct reports— they usually spend very little time on individual contributor work. Despite these differences, they all add value as leaders, so they are all required to have the work values, time application, and skills as outlined in this chapter.

Let's examine some of the differences that we have experienced in our work with companies.

Store Managers (Retail)

In the retail companies we have worked with, we have found that they benefit from operating with two types of leaders-of-others roles with different sets of leadership expectations: one for the traditional leaders-of-others in different regional and headquarters functions and one for the store managers.

What is significantly different about these two roles is the type of leadership work they need to spend time on and the skills that are most important.

Given the high turnover of employees in stores, the store managers spend much more time on recruitment and onboarding of new employees. However, the jobs in a store are usually prede-fined and hence job design becomes less important. Even though they may lead 20 or 30 part-time or full-time employees, they participate very actively in individual contributor work when needed. They place groceries on the shelves, they clean up, they arrange the merchandise, and in rush hour they may take a turn at the cash register. Day-to-day planning and weekly planning become much more important than annual planning. The time horizon is simply shorter. The store is open many more hours than they work, so they often have an assistant store manager whom they essentially have to train in their own job so they can take over. Every day, every week, every month they get all kinds of data so they can see how the store is performing. Employees usually don't have individual business objectives except for some in clothing retail, where they may be measured on individual sales. They don't spend the same amount of time on setting objectives as some other versions of leaders-of-others.

Retail companies benefit from developing specific leadership expectations and work values, time application, and skills for this role.

Supervisors (Manufacturing)

When we implement the Leadership Pipeline concept in manufacturing organizations, we are often met with the comment: "We will not apply this to our supervisors; they are not leaders in the same way." Our response is, of course they are completely right. Supervisors are not leaders in "the same way." The nature of the leadership job of supervisor on a manufacturing site is quite different from a leader-of-others in an office setting. However, they are indeed leaders-of-others, and they typically lead 5 or 10 times as many employees as any office leader-of-others does. Hence, defining that leadership role is as relevant.

What is often special about the manufacturing supervisor role is that they might lead 30 to 60 employees. Often their employees work in shifts. The supervisor must make sure that the operation works flawlessly whether they are present or not. Accordingly, they often design self-leading teams. These are teams in which some of the employees are given responsibility for onboarding new employees, planning vacations, handling day-to-day conflicts, running team whiteboard meetings, and so on. The supervisor then has to train the teams and the employees in these roles as part of their own operational role.

The supervisor doesn't have the same type of career discussions with their employees. Most of their employees will have careers on the manufacturing floor. They rarely set individual objectives. They rally their employees around the factory goals and the team goals for important activities such as quality, productivity, and safety. Also, they don't negotiate salary with each employee, and they don't manage individual bonus schemes; added to this, the workplace may be unionized, which requires the supervisor to keep these agreements in mind when carrying out their leadership duties such as recruitment, performance reviews, and dismissals. Quite often, supervisors are full-time leaders. They don't have a designated role in production. They may step in during any emergency.

The job design is pretty much given but motivating people and setting the climate, however, become crucial parts of their role.

All in all, it is hard to argue against including the manufacturing supervisor role when designing the leadership pipeline architecture in manufacturing organizations.

Leaders-of-Others Who Are Also Specialists

Case study

In a large international construction and maintenance company, we sat with the chief product officer (CPO) and the global head of learning and development (GH L&D). We were in the process of mapping the leadership and specialist roles within the top four layers. At one point in the conversation, we got to discuss the GH L&D role. The GH L&D had a small team of four employees. The company was globally divided into four regions: North America, South America, Europe, and Asia Pacific. In each region, they had a learning and development director (L&D director). The region L&D director reported to the regional head of human resources—not the GH L&D.

The CPO asked this question: "Is the GH L&D role a knowledge leader role or a leader-of-others role? I appreciate that she is leading four people and from that perspective, she is certainly a leader-of-others. However, her primary role isn't to lead these four people. Leading these four people is the easy part of the job. Her primary role is to be our knowledge leader representing the domain of leadership development and to drive results through the regional L&D directors without having the formal authority to make things happen."

The CPO is quite right in his reflections. Within central support functions in particular, many leaders-of-others should operate as knowledge experts or knowledge leaders even though they lead a small team. This is how it works in reality, but most organizations pigeonhole people into either one role or the other. The comment we often hear is, "Operating with combined roles adds too much complexity." Our response is always, "It doesn't *add* complexity, it simply creates transparency on the *already existing* complexity within your organization."

We experience the same situations in many knowledge-based organizations. Most of their leaders-of-others only have three or four direct reports, and the leaders are appointed team leaders due to their specialist knowledge. The consequence is that they spend as little as one-quarter of their time on leadership work. Accordingly, they have the same leadership job that needs to get done as any other leader-of-others. However, they spend much more time on horizontal leadership, managing stakeholders, liaising with external partners, and keeping on top of the latest developments within their domain of expertise. These elements need to be added to the leadership expectations and work values, time application, and skills for this role.

Project Leaders

In our encounters with large project organizations, we have experienced some very good project management training. However, in addition to these core tools and skills they get from this training, they still need to transition into their leadership role.

The key difference between a project leader and the line leader-of-others is not so much the job that needs to get done or the required work values, time application, and skills. The difference relates to the fact that they only do part of the leadership work for the project members. The other parts are performed by the line leader.

Cutting the "leadership cake" between the project manager and the line manager is a big topic in many organizations. Accordingly, we have chosen to address this challenge more completely in Chapter 11.

We could have listed many more examples. The main point is, you can apply the Leadership Portrait of a leader-of-others as outlined in this chapter and then build on that by describing your organization-specific leadership roles.

4

Leading Leaders

Though most organizations have training programs for first-line leaders, relatively few have any programs in place for leaders-of-leaders. Part of the problem is the false assumption that there's very little difference between leading others and leading leaders—the logic being that if you can develop the skills of a first-line leader, you will naturally adapt to this similar, but more significant, role. The other aspect of the problem is psychological, in that promotion to this position is often viewed as a stepping-stone rather than a major career transition. Whereas being appointed as a first-line leader is a cause for celebration, the move to a leader-of-leaders is usually greeted with more muted enthusiasm.

Yet there is a significant difference in work values, time applications, and skills for this leadership layer versus the leader-of-others. They are supposed to select and develop the leaders-of-others and hold them accountable for leading. If this transition isn't addressed, many leadership contributions are missed, much to the detriment of their organization. The leader-of-leaders usually does the work of the leaders-of-others when they don't transition properly. Short term, the workforce is confused and poorly or inadequately led.

Leaders-of-leaders are responsible for the vast majority of people in the company. They lead the leaders-of-others and the hands-on people who get the organization's products and services produced and delivered. As you can imagine, quality and productivity suffer when leaders-of-leaders aren't performing their roles effectively. In fact, errors here harm an organization's ability to execute and may even create a competitive disadvantage.

Identifying leaders who are experiencing difficulty with this passage is easier than finding leaders who have been successful. An interesting observation from our executive succession planning work since the 1980s is that one of the most common reasons for senior executives struggling in their role is that they never developed the skills required for the leader-of-leaders role. Time itself does not solve the problem. The problem only grows bigger.

The Job to Be Done

In Figure 4.1 we've summarized a fundamental performance portrait for the leading leaders layer. Later in this chapter, we discuss how the role of leaders-of-leaders can differ based on industry, organizational structure, and business model. What we are outlining is the job to be done in most leading leaders roles. However, it is not a job description, and you should customize it to fit your organization's needs and the operating results to be delivered.

To elaborate on each category of work in turn: a leader-of-leaders gets the team to value leadership work.

Leaders-of-Leaders Translate Strategy into Operating Plans

They take steps to ensure they have a clear picture of the business strategy and how their part of the organization contributes to it. Then they break down the strategy into deliverables for each of their teams, making sure that there is a clear line of sight between frontline activities and the overall strategy. Technical and professional employees are now expressing serious dissatisfaction with their jobs if they don't see this important connection.

Assigning work, defining deliverables, and delegating authority are major requirements. To ensure smooth execution, leaders-of-

The Work	Required Activities
Translate strategy into operating plans	• Create a clear line of sight between front line activities and the overall business strategy. • Support front line leaders making meaning of the business strategy. • Assign work and delegate necessary decision-power to direct reports.
Develop leaders	• Take a structured approach to support your leaders becoming better leaders. • Coach direct reports on leadership in everyday life. • Support direct reports in developing their functional expertise.
Follow through on performance of leaders	• Give direct reports a fact-based assessment on how well they perform as leaders. • Give direct reports a fact-based assessment on how well they perform on their business objective. • Include feed-back on leadership performance in ongoing check-in conversations.
Select leaders	• Select new leaders based on leadership potential – not just functional expertise. • Select direct reports for tomorrow – not just today. • Replace direct reports who consistently fall short of fulfilling their leadership role.
Build the organization	• Align organizational capabilities with both operational and strategic needs of the business. • Build a diverse organization. • Establish reliable succession plans.
Lead across the organization	• Take a holistic approach in driving value across the organization. • Break down silos and facilitate a free flow of information and ideas across teams. • Stimulate collaboration across the value chain.

Figure 4.1. Leading Leaders: The Job to Be Done.
Source: Copyright Leadership Pipeline Institute.

leaders delegate the appropriate amount of authority to their direct reports so results are delivered on time. If responsibilities and authority are not aligned, the leader-of-leaders easily becomes the bottleneck.

Even the best strategy runs into challenges. Parts of the strategy may have to be postponed or some temporary initiatives are taken that are not completely supporting the strategy. Whenever these things happen, employees may become cynical about the strategy. Leaders-of-leaders need to constantly be on top of any changes taking place in the business in order to explain them to their organization. They are the advocates for top management in these cases. This can be tough, but it is part of having a well-functioning middle management.

Leaders-of-Leaders Develop Other Leaders

Becoming skilled in developing leaders-of-others requires a certain amount of experience. It takes a while to realize how to set goals that require growth but don't cause failure. It is important to support the frontline leaders in developing their own leadership style rather than forcing a specific style on them. Leaders-of-leaders may ask themselves, "Why don't they just do it the way I did it?" There can be many excellent reasons and they should be explored.

Training first-line leaders requires creating a supportive environment that allows mistakes but not failure. It's an environment in which there's great enthusiasm for learning. To foster this environment, leaders-of-leaders need to develop a sensitivity about power. This means they need to use their power in ways that motivate and coach rather than demean and demoralize. More than one boss has reflexively reacted to a first-line leader's mistake by making them feel powerless. Balancing positive and negative feedback and recognizing the best time to deliver negative feedback or feed-forward and knowing how to deliver it are hallmarks of a good leader-of-leaders.

Leaders-of-Leaders Follow Through on the Performance of Other Leaders

This calls for shifting their accountability attention because previously they focused on holding people responsible for individual contributor/technical work. In this role they need to learn how to hold first-line leaders accountable for leadership work: the quality of their selection decisions, the frequency and quality of their performance feedback, their coaching, their ability to team with other units, and their skill at producing results through a team.

Leaders-of-Leaders Select Leaders

Selecting leaders is a task foreign to new leaders-of-others. They're not used to evaluating factors such as an individual's willingness to lead, communication and planning skills, ability to motivate and drive engagement, and work values. This means identifying people who are likely candidates and giving them the opportunity to see whether they like and are good at leadership work. Giving people team leadership and project leadership assignments are just two of many ways to learn about a person's ability and willingness to lead.

Leaders-of-leaders need to remove first-line leaders who don't make the grade. In many instances, this is a more difficult task than removing an individual contributor. Whereas the reason for removing an individual contributor is usually more clear-cut—they aren't delivering needed results or they don't fit this company's values—the reasons for moving a first-line leader sideways or out are less tangible. Failing to perform leadership duties and not spending enough time on them are common reasons. Recognizing these problems and taking people out of leadership roles requires some courage, emotional fortitude, and self-confidence. Allowing underperforming leaders to remain in first-line leadership jobs clogs the leadership pipeline at its source; it also can rob the company of high-performing individual contributors. No one wants to work for a bad leader.

Leaders-of-Leaders Build a Diverse Organization

This is an important requirement because it means choosing contributors over clones. Too often we experience leaders-of-leaders choosing people with whom they have an established relationship or former direct reports over people who are truly best qualified for the leadership position. This tactic can be a disaster because these friends are often unwilling to challenge their boss and might not bring fresh perspectives to the job. Not paying attention to diversity is a mistake.

Leaders-of-Leaders Lead Across the Organization

This means managing the boundaries between teams reporting to them and between peer organizations. They must understand where their work comes from and where it goes. This is a critical accountability. They are silo-busters who tear down any walls that impede the flow of work and information across different functions and other groups. This of course means transitioning from a purely operational mindset to a mindset that embraces total business results. Just as important, they must inculcate this value among first-line leaders and individual contributors. Effective cross-unit collaboration usually accelerates work processes, and strong leaders-of-leaders help their organization gain this competitive advantage. Managing boundaries is a matter of values and workflow management skills. This means monitoring the flow of work between their unit and others in the organization, asking questions, and recommending improvements.

The Transition to the Role

It is easy for leaders to miss the required transition from leading others to leading leaders. If they think they now just lead more people, they will be terribly wrong. Often, leaders-of-leaders have been promoted into their role without any transition support. The organization simply believes the leader in question seemed to be well prepared for a leader-of-leaders role based on many years of good performance in leading others. Highly skilled, conscientious leaders-of-others can easily look as if they can step into a leader-of-leaders' role without missing a beat. Appearances can be especially deceiving at this level. The leader-of-leaders role is very different from the leader-of-others role. It is a completely different job.

If an organization does not operate with a clear set of differentiated portraits for leaders-of-others versus leaders-of-leaders, and the associated set of work values, time application, and skills, then it is asking for trouble.

Figure 4.2 offers an overview of the core difference in work values, time application, and skills between leaders-of-others and leaders-of-leaders. The list represents what applies to most leader-of-leaders roles. Your organization may need to add to these.

Leading Others

WORK VALUES
- Achieving results through others
- Success of direct reports and unit
- Self as leader

TIME APPLICATION
- Annual planning (budget, projects)
- Making time available for direct reports
- Managerial work

SKILLS
- Job design
- Selecting
- Delegating
- Coaching
- Giving feedback
- Performance management
- Building engagement
- Building the team
- Building psychological safety

Leading Leaders

WORK VALUES
- Achieving results through leaders
- Success in value chain
- Ambiguity
- Values based leadership

TIME APPLICATION
- Long-term (two to three years) operational planning
- Resource allocation
- Providing input upwards for strategy planning
- Managing boundaries between teams
- Managing boundaries to peer organizations

SKILLS
- Organizational design
- Selecting leaders
- Managing stakeholders
- Coaching of leaders
- Assessing performance of leaders
- Building a diverse organization
- Building agility within the organization
- Strategic capability building

Figure 4.2. Leading Others Versus Leading Leaders: Core Differences in Work Values, Time Application, and Skills.

Source: Copyright Leadership Pipeline Institute.

What were the two or three main challenges you faced during the first three to six months after moving into your leader-of-leaders role?	What two or three things do you miss most about being a leader-of-others or an individual contributor?	What two or three things would you like to spend more time on in your current position, but seem unable to find time for?	What are the two or three most important skills you have come to realize you need as a leader-of-others?

1. Losing control from not knowing everything in depth
 	
2. Clarity on position in value chain–how does my organization fit into the bigger picture
 	
3. Communicating through leaders–there is a delay from when I brief my team until things happens in the frontline
 	
4. Managing stakeholders
 	
5. Being hands-off–trusting the team
	1. Being close to the action– the satisfaction of completing a task
	
	2. Being an expert in my work area
	
	3. Having the detailed overview – knowing where are we?
	
	4. Time control:
	  a. single/multiple tasks
	  b. grabbed by others
	  c. control over deadlines
	
	5. Work-life balance
		1. Focusing on strategy rather than putting out fires
		
		2. Understanding company strategy
		
		3. Networking/ knowledge sharing with peers
		
		4. Long-term planning – being less reactive
		
		5. Being more visible to my own organization – rather than just to my direct reports
			1. Leading through other leaders
			
			2. Stakeholder management – relationship building
			
			3. Assessing my leaders – how do I know if they are good leaders?
			
			4. Empowering my teams to get things done without my interference
			
			5. Coaching leaders

Figure 4.3. Consolidated Results for Leaders-of-Leaders.
Source: Copyright Leadership Pipeline Institute.

In Chapter 1 we described our action research done since 2010. In Figure 4.3 you see the consolidated results for leaders-of-leaders.

Work Values

The leading leaders is a much purer leadership position. Some leaders-of-leaders lead only small organizations of 15 people, but most lead organizations of 30, 50, or 100 people. In these big organizations, they seldom do any individual contributor work.

No matter what size the organization might be, becoming an effective leader-of-others starts by adopting the right mindset. The first thought each day should be, "I am building leaders and connecting them." Leadership development in any organization starts with leaders-of-leaders, not training programs. Efficiency is built by all leaders-of-others being connected so that work flows seamlessly across the organization.

Case study

Miguel works in the R&D function of a luxury consumer electronics company. He has for many years been recognized in his leader-of-others roles for developing high-performing and highly talented specialists. Eighteen months ago, he was promoted to a leader-of-leaders position due to his ability to attract, retain, and develop people. In the new role, Miguel was leading three former peers who were all in leader-of-others roles. Within these 18 months, two former peers had resigned from the company and one had moved to another function within the company. Deadlines were being missed. All of this frustrated Ahn, the head of the R&D function.

Consequently, Ahn asked the HR function to look into the situation. Her first take was that the peers had felt bypassed in the promotion process and she wanted to avoid that in the future. After looking into the situation, the HR function came up with a somewhat different conclusion. The exit interviews with the two leaders-of-others who left the company and conversations with the current leaders-of-others reporting to Miguel painted a clear picture of a Miguel, who, in many ways, treated the leaders-of-others as specialists rather than leaders-of-others. No effort was being made to build teamwork or leadership skills.

In this case, Miguel had taken leading-others strengths and used them in the leader-of-leaders role. He had always been good at developing specialists, coaching them, and giving feedback. But in the new role, the direct reports expected to be developed as leaders. When selecting new leaders-of-others, the sole focus was on people's professional expertise rather than also taking leadership potential into consideration. Rather than forming a leadership team with his direct reports, he preferred leading them one-on-one and often joined the meeting they had with their teams. All in all, Miguel simply did not value leading through other leaders, supporting them in becoming better leaders, and allowing them to be team leaders in their own right. In this specific case, Ahn eventually moved Miguel back to a team leader role, though, leading a significantly larger team than previously.

Time Application

As mentioned previously, the leader-of-leaders role is a much purer leadership role with consequences for poor time application. Leaders-of-others with teams consisting of fewer than 10 employees may still spend a good part of their time on individual contributor work. However, leaders-of-leaders should not be involved much—if at all—in individual contributor work. At this level, the role is to get things done through the leaders reporting to them. Some leaders-of-leaders also have senior specialists reporting directly to them. In these structures they must enable the senior specialists to get their work done across the organization as required without interference.

Most leaders-of-leaders have seven or fewer direct reports. How can they spend their entire day "leading"? It is correct that the downward leadership role does not take the entire day. However, leaders-of-leaders also play an important role in tying the organization together horizontally. They need to set aside considerable time to connect across the organization. Managing the boundaries between their own unit and peer units, managing stakeholders across the organization, and participating in various cross-functional projects all take time. Furthermore, many leading leaders are involved in providing input upward to inform the strategy process. They need to dedicate time to getting a complete understanding of the strategy because they are responsible for translating it into operational plans.

Many leaders-of-leaders are surprised by how much time the horizontal part of their leadership role takes. We often hear comments such as "I feel that I am taken away from my organization,"

"I will never get my job done if I have to spend so much time away from my unit," or "I am part of so many meetings outside my own organization." However, this is the nature of the leading-leaders role. It simply goes with the job. Consequently leaders-of-leaders do not have time to conduct individual contributor work.

Skills

At a first glance, some of the required leading-leaders skills appear similar to the leaders-of-others skills. For instance, leaders-of-others coach their employees, as do leaders-of-leaders. Leaders-of-others assess the performance of direct reports, as do leaders-of-leaders. Leaders-of-others select people and build their team, as do leaders-of-leaders. And after all, these are the major time-consuming parts of being a leader—so what is really the difference?

That is indeed a fair question, but the answer is very simple: there are major differences, and not recognizing these differences is one of the biggest mistakes a new leader can make.

Table 4.1 illustrates the difference between the two roles within three areas that are more subtle—and thus often neglected.

When moving into a leader-of-leaders role, leadership becomes the profession. The major pitfall related to these three skills is focusing on technical/professional proficiencies when they select, develop, and assess performance of their direct reports who are leading others. Doing that, they will not only end up struggling with their own performance but also they will cause the entire leadership pipeline to be clogged. The new skill is the ability to judge and improve the way their direct reports do things such as setting direction, coaching, assigning work, and measuring performance.

Table 4.1. Three Differences Between Leaders-of-Others and Leaders-of-Leaders.

Leaders-of-Others	Leaders-of-Leaders
Select individual contributors	Select leaders
Develop individual contributors	Develop leaders
Assess performance of individual contributors	Assess performance of leaders

Typical Transition Issues

For most people, moving from a leader-of-others role to a leader-of-leaders role is associated with significant challenges. Let's review the typical pitfalls using some examples. (See Figure 4.4.)

Neglecting to Develop Direct Reports into Effective Leaders

We met with an organization that for several years had worked on building a leader-led development culture. Essentially, they wanted all leaders to assume responsibility for developing their direct reports on the job in everyday work life.

They had implemented a range of different initiatives in order to achieve the objectives:

- All leaders were offered training in coaching.

- All leaders went through e-learning in 70–20–10 principles, setting effective development objectives and other relevant topics.

Typical Transition Issues

- Neglecting to develop direct reports into effective leaders
- Neglecting to explicitly hold direct reports accountable for leadership performance
- Failing to truly empower the leaders reporting to them
- Focusing mainly on leading downwards but not much on leading sideways and upwards
- Struggling with the combination of individual contributors and leaders-of-others as direct reports

Figure 4.4. Typical Transition Issues for Leaders-of-Leaders.
Source: Copyright Leadership Pipeline Institute.

- The organization implemented a special feature in the performance and development system, allowing the HR function to measure if all employees had at least one development objective.

- In the engagement survey, they followed up specifically on questions related to whether people felt they developed in their job. This included a quarterly pulse survey in which a percentage of employees were asked questions related to development in their job.

After a couple of years, they had significantly improved their learning culture. However, we were contacted because they still faced problems in developing a sufficient number of qualified leaders, especially at the frontline leader level.

Through our diagnostics, we were able to disclose the challenge. Some of the questions we asked a selected number of leaders-of-others were the following:

- In the past three one-on-one conversations with your direct manager, how much time percentage-wise was spent on making you a better leader versus discussing numbers, milestones, technical challenges, or simple problem-solving?

- What percentage of your development objectives are focused on making you a better leader?

- To what extent do you experience that you are explicitly held accountable for being a good leader?

There were several other questions, and they were combined with collecting specific development objectives and interviewing a selected number of leaders at different leadership levels.

The findings from the small diagnostic exercise were very consistent. Whereas all leaders focused more on the development of direct reports compared to what we usually see, the leaders-of-leaders were primarily focused on developing the professional skills of the team leaders rather than developing leadership skills. The lack of leadership development was caused mostly by two factors: (1) The leaders-of-leaders did not know how to develop leaders on the job, so they fell back to what they used to do as leaders-of-others—namely, developing their direct reports' professional skills, and (2) the leaders-of-leaders did not value this part of their role. Intellectually, they appreciated the importance of it, but in everyday life, they never carved out time for it.

Neglecting to Explicitly Hold Direct Reports Accountable for Leadership Performance

When we apply our leadership diagnostic tool with clients, we ask leaders-of-leaders how important it is to them that their direct reports perform well as leaders. The average rating on a 10-point scale is 9.5.

We also ask leaders-of-others reporting to the same leaders-of-leaders: "To what extent on a 10-point scale do you experience explicitly being held accountable for being a good leader?" The average rating on this question is 5.

Why would leaders-of-leaders, who consider good leadership critical for them, not explicitly hold their leaders-of-others accountable for their leadership performance?

As previously discussed, most leaders-of-leaders were promoted to their role from a leader-of-others position. As leaders-of-others, they hold direct reports accountable for their technical results, professional work, and professional proficiencies. What we witness from the diagnostic work is simply that leaders-of-leaders continue to operate as leaders-of-others when reviewing the performances of their direct reports.

Intellectually, the leaders-of-leaders appreciate the importance of having good leaders reporting to them, so they have transitioned somewhat with regard to work values. But they are not dedicating sufficient time to gather performance facts, which can be time-consuming. Facts about leadership performance cannot, similar to many business results, be automatically tracked with a system. There is no substitute for getting out into the organization and seeing people in action. Skills for capturing performance facts and interpreting them correctly are essential to this role.

Case study

Hired by a large technology corporation to be a manager of software development and conversion, Vic moved from running a software application unit and managing 14 people to being responsible for 150 people, with 12 direct reports whose work units developed, purchased, and maintained existing software. Vic's new employer faced significant conversion challenges, deadlines, and competitive pressures.

As a first-line manager, Vic possessed the right stuff. Not only had he gone through a good training program but also he'd used 360-degree feedback to increase his understanding of his managerial strengths and weaknesses, and he worked assiduously to correct flaws. In his new role, Vic spent a great deal of time learning about all the projects in his domain and getting to know the people. During this learning phase, Vic discovered that several important projects were behind schedule, that he was a better first-line manager than many of his direct reports, and that morale was low because people were working overtime without much success.

With the decisiveness and skill that had made him a good first-line manager, Vic quickly took action. By conducting project reviews, reordering priorities, and reassigning applications specialists, he made some modest improvements. However, these improvements weren't significant enough to satisfy Vic

(continued)

and his boss. Furthermore, he was drowning in people problems. A line formed at Vic's door first thing every morning as his direct reports and individual contributors sought his input and approval. Soon Vic didn't have the time he needed to deal with the budget and project issues that needed addressing.

Failing to Truly Empower the Leaders Reporting to Them

The major focus of leaders-of-leaders—the area from which work values, time application, and skills all flow—is empowering first-line managers. Instead of empowering them, Vic was disenfranchising them. By giving direct orders to individual contributors and conducting his own project reviews, Vic was taking over activities that rightly belonged to his direct reports. Individual contributors began to bypass their own bosses to talk to Vic, because he was obviously running everything.

If Vic had the help he needed to properly transitioned to this leadership level, he would have responded very differently to this situation. Right from the start, he would have assembled his team, listened to their viewpoints, and pushed for recommendations. Although Vic certainly could have exercised his veto power if recommendations were inappropriate, he also could have let first-line managers choose from the options available. By giving his people the power to make project decisions and holding them accountable for these decisions, Vic would have created a better setting for his direct reports to develop leadership skills. He would have avoided his own time crunch.

Vic also would have time to observe how his managers managed. Rather than treat them as individual contributors doing technical work, he would have treated and assessed them as leaders doing leadership work. By paying attention to his direct reports' leadership work values, time application, and skills, Vic would have gathered the information necessary for him to coach them effectively.

Focusing Mainly on Leading Downwards but Not Much on Leading Sideways and Upwards

Take another look at Figure 4.3 in the third column: "What two or three things would you like to spend more time on in your current position but seem unable to find time for?" You will notice two findings:

- Understanding company strategy

- Networking/knowledge sharing with peers

All the leaders-of-leaders we have met are busy—very busy. They work hard with long hours. So any solution to their problems can't come from working additional hours. No matter what they do, they will usually never have time to do all the things they would like to do. The trick is to strike the right balance and empower their direct reports as leaders.

A consumer electronics company with about 1,800 employees had very low scores among frontline employees in their engagement survey. The two lowest-scoring questions were these:

- Do you understand our company strategy?

- Do you understand how your work is tied into our company strategy?

They also faced low scores in a number of related questions. Some representative comments from the frontline employees were these:

- "We seem to be changing the strategy several times during the year, so we don't really have a strategy."

- "I don't see any logic between the strategy we have on paper and how we prioritize our work in everyday life."

- "I am not sure that my manager understands the strategy."

The immediate response from top management was to increase the number of town hall meetings from one annual meeting to quarterly meetings. Their rationale was, "We need to be closer to the frontline employees and better explain our strategy."

This did not help the scores.

When we were invited in, we started by interviewing the layer of leaders between top management and the frontline leaders. We quickly realized that the problem originated with this layer of leaders—the leaders-of-leaders.

There is a long distance between a company strategy and frontline activities. They needed the leaders-of-leaders to understand and embrace the strategy and then translate the strategy into operational plans and ensure a clear line of sight between strategic goals and everyday activities.

Also, even with the best strategy in place, companies may need to make decisions during the year that are not directly supporting the strategy and sometimes decisions that may even be viewed as contradicting it. This is the nature of running a business in a fast-changing business environment. The role of leaders-of-leaders in these situations is to help the frontline managers and frontline employees to understand the rationale behind these decisions. To do so, they need to spend time themselves learning the strategic situation, rather than just executing it.

Even though there were only about 25 middle managers, the middle managers had never created a forum where they could meet and discuss cross-functional matters. Some did meet, but mainly on one-and-one conversations and in a fairly unstructured way.

In this specific company, though, the middle managers did not get much support when stepping into their role. Top management was frequently "pushing" the middle managers downward in the organization by holding them directly accountable for producing all kinds of detailed information. Likewise, they had never defined the middle manager role as a distinct role. They merely treated them as "big" leaders-of-others. We also saw how the top management, after realizing the low engagement scores, took it on themselves to push the strategy down in the organization themselves instead of mobilizing the leaders-of-leaders.

This is also what makes this case important. When looking for the root cause of the problem, look carefully before drawing conclusions. In this case, it would have been easy to conclude the root cause was the leaders-of-leaders primarily leading downward. However, the way top management understood and used the leaders-of-leaders role was actually the root cause.

Struggling with the Combination of Individual Contributors and Leaders-of-Others as Direct Reports

Sometimes we experience organizations where the organizational design is very simple with clear structures. In retail, for instance, we see all store managers (leaders-of-others) reporting to district managers (leaders-of-leaders), district managers reporting to regional managers (leaders-of-leaders leading other leaders-of-leaders), and regional managers reporting to the chief operating officer (the function manager). We see similar simple organizational designs in manufacturing.

In these cases, the leaders-of-leaders only have other leaders reporting to them and that makes perfect sense. However, this is far from the reality for many leaders-of-leaders. Many leaders-of-leaders have both leaders-of-others and individual contributors reporting to them. For all practical purposes, this means they have two leadership roles to play. When they have a one-on-one check-in conversation with one of their team leaders, they need to assume the role of leaders-of-leaders. But two hours later, they may have a one-on-one check-in conversation with one of their individual contributors. Then they need to assume the leading-others role.

We often see leaders-of-leaders struggling to balance these two parts of their role. It is challenging to transition from leading others to leading leaders and really stepping up to that role. It does not make it any easier if you are also leading others. However, that is simply the reality, and what we see is a tendency for leaders-of-leaders in this situation to end up treating everyone as individual contributors. The consequences are quite visible.

The business objectives for the leaders-of-others are set at too low a level; the leaders-of-others find the required authority is not delegated to them; the leaders-of-others do not have any development objectives related to making them better leaders, and the leaders-of-others are only held accountable for individual contributor work rather than their leadership performance.

Variations of the Role

Just like the leading others role, the leading leaders role can vary from industry to industry. In knowledge-based organizations, many leaders-of-leaders will have team leaders and high-level specialists reporting to them. In large, highly operational organizations, there may be two or three layers of leaders-of-leaders. Accordingly, some leaders-of-leaders may lead an organization of 25 people, whereas others lead an organization with hundreds of employees. Despite these differences, they must add value as leaders-of-leaders, so they are all subject to the work values, time application, and skills as outlined in this chapter.

Leaders-of-Leaders in Technology

Many leaders-of-leaders have both individual contributors and leaders-of-others reporting to them. This is common in technology-based organizations and scientific organizations. These organizations must ensure that their high-level specialists are not pushed down in the organization. They should be lifted up in the organization to ensure that their voice and knowledge are represented in the leadership teams. That is leader-of-others work.

How should these leaders be categorized, as leaders-of-others or leaders-of-leaders? It is important to remember that the Leadership Pipeline is not a hierarchical model; it is a role-based leadership model. You are not either/or—you are both! Their time allocation is usually the determining factor when deciding what training should be given or what rewards are appropriate.

When having a one-on-one meeting with a specialist, they are doing the work of a leader-of-others. But when they meet with one of the team leaders reporting to them, they must do leader-of-leaders work. This is not easy. Those leaders-of-leaders should think carefully about the guidance they give to specialists.

Leaders-of-Leaders in Manufacturing

At the end of Chapter 3 we described how the leader-of-others role in manufacturing organizations is often considered to be a supervisor, not a leader. We conclude that supervisors should be viewed as leaders-of-others even though there are certain parts of the leaders-of-others role that they don't do; activities such as job design, salary discussions, hiring, firing, and setting individual business objectives are not always part of a supervisor's role.

Accordingly, many leaders-of-leaders in manufacturing find themselves involved in what might be classed as leaders-of-others work in other organizations. There is nothing wrong with that. Just make sure that, when defining the leader-of-leaders role in manufacturing, the description of the job to be done and the work values, time application, and skills all reflect leading leaders requirements.

We have used manufacturing as the example here. This often applies in large shared service centers, retail organizations, and delivery companies where there are large numbers of hourly workers with union contracts in place.

Leaders-of-Leaders Can Be Section Leaders

Even in an era of delayering, we see that in large companies it is not uncommon to have two or even three layers of leaders-of-leaders. There is nothing wrong with that. It is all about how you best organize to execute the strategy, accommodate distance, and lead large numbers of people.

Not distinguishing between these layers is where problems start. They should be playing different roles. If they do not play different roles, it would be better to eliminate one of the layers. If they do play different roles, it might be helpful to call the higher layer of leaders-of-leaders *section leaders*.

In Chapter 11, we have dedicated space to address how to define these two roles set side by side and what really makes the difference when you select people for each of the roles.

We could have listed many more examples. The main point is, you can apply the core role description of a leader-of-leaders outlined in this chapter and then build on that by adding organization-specific leadership work.

On a closing note, it is, however, important to stress that, irrespective of the different types of leaders-of-leaders, your main source for creating value is to get things done through highly capable leaders.

5

Leading a Function

When people are promoted to the function leader role, they are excited to be at the top of the profession in their business. They report to a business leader directly (who may also be the CEO) and are part of the business team. Their peers are now the other function leaders.

The business leader in most cases is not a product of the same function, so there won't be much technical guidance for the new function manager, but there will be business guidance. That business guidance must be translated into function plans. In turn, function managers provide guidance to the business leader on the function's capability and state-of-the-art so the business leader can make informed and sound strategic decisions.

The primary purpose of a function leader is to give their business a competitive edge by delivering function capability and results that are better than their competitors. As such, the business achieves its goals and improves its competitive position through the ability of each function to deliver.

Being an integral part of the business team, participating in the development of business strategy, and building a function competitive edge are top priorities. Being part of the business team and being responsible for the function delivering a competitive edge makes this role completely different from any leadership role in that function. Many leaders are successfully working in lower-level leadership roles within the function. Only a select few will be successful in the function leader role, because it requires a transition from operational thinking and planning to strategic thinking and planning. Emotional maturity is an important transition requirement because these leaders now lead their former peers and friends.

We know there can be confusion about this role, so we will start by defining what we mean, in the Leadership Pipeline model, by the term *function leader*.

The Definition of the Role

There are many big differences between the function leader role versus other leadership roles within a function. Function leaders are responsible for setting the function's direction, for producing function strategy, and for building the function's capability. Because they report directly to the business leader or the enterprise leader, they provide function expertise to the business team. Accordingly, their peers are now other function heads. In many instances, their peers from when they were leaders-of-leaders now report to them.

Depending on variables such as size, industry practices, and geographic footprint, some typical functions are manufacturing/operations, supply chain, sales, marketing, R&D, engineering, IT, finance, HR, legal, audit, and procurement.

We have experienced that some organizations use the *function leader* term for a variety of roles. This is partly due to various business trends, consultancy ideas, and a mix of role definition versus title definition. Any organization can, of course, name roles in whatever way works best for them.

Small and mid-size companies are frequently organized as just one business with one business leader who is also the enterprise leader. This can also be the situation for large companies built on one product line or one family of products or services. In such a

Figure 5.1. Likely Enterprise Organization Structure in a Single-Business Company.
Source: Copyright Leadership Pipeline Institute.

case, there may only be 5 to 10 function leaders in the entire company. (See Figure 5.1.)

Other companies have multiple business units (BUs), and each BU has its own business leader and function leaders. (See Figure 5.2.) The enterprise leader usually has function leaders who have enterprise accountability.

In Figure 5.2, the BU function leaders often have a dotted line to the group function leader. (Please note that some organizations use the term *group* functions, whereas others use *corporate* functions. They mean the same thing.) With four BUs, there are four BU CFOs and one group CFO. The job to be done in a BU function leader role is different from the group function leader role; we will discuss the main differences later on.

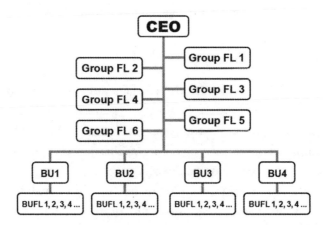

Figure 5.2. Likely Enterprise Organization Structure in a Multiple-Business Company.
Source: Copyright Leadership Pipeline Institute.

One indicator of a function leader role is reporting directly to the business leader or CEO. This is not always the case. When business leaders and CEOs decide how they will be organized, they choose how many and which functions they want to have reporting directly to them. For instance, some CEOs and business leaders have an aggregation person (COO, CFO, etc.) who oversees legal, public relations, procurement, and sometimes HR. Often, we see the CFO having several different functions reporting to them, such as IT and legal. These aggregated elements (legal, IT, PR, and so on) are still functions.

It may help you in understanding who the function leaders are by understanding who are not function leaders.

The head of tax reporting to the head of accounting, the head of talent reporting to the CHRO, the head of IT security reporting to the head of IT, and so on, are sometimes called function leaders. These roles do not lead an entire function. They lead a practice within a function but aren't asked to produce a function strategy. If you want a distinct label for them, you may want to name them practice leaders. But they are not function leaders. Often, their role is a combination of a leader-of-others and leader-of-leaders role with a specialist role at the knowledge leader level. There is a difference between titles and roles. The Leadership Pipeline is focused on roles.

The Job to Be Done

In Figure 5.3, we summarize the fundamental job to be done in most function leader roles. However, it is not a job description, and you should customize it to your organization. We don't include operating results, for example. The specific job content requires the incumbent to develop and execute function strategy, contribute to business strategy, and advise on function capability as a member of the business team, drive function excellence, build the function's operating model, and take ownership of function talent. All of this is done for the business.

The Work	Required Activities
Help the business team succeed	• Participate actively in defining and executing the overall business strategy. • Acknowledge the value of other functions. • Take cross-functional concerns into consideration in discussions and decision-making rather than only considering own function.
Develop and execute functional strategy	• Develop a functional strategy that supports the overall business strategy. • Push the functional agenda into the future, seeking short- and long-term competitive advantages. • Execute the functional strategy timely and effectively.
Drive functional excellence	• Implement and optimize key functional processes timely and thoroughly. • Create an innovative environment that inspires new ways of working. • Establish relevant key performance indicators for the function.
Build the function	• Build the function to meet short-term and long-term business needs. • Implement a functional system/rhythm. • Establish an organizational structure that allows function-wide initiatives to reach the rest of the organization at the desired speed.
Take ownership of developing functional talent	• Identify long-term and short-term successors at all levels of the function. • Create space within the function for talents to develop. • Cooperate with functional peers to secure cross-function development opportunities for talents.
Develop leaders	• Take a structured approach to support your leaders becoming better leaders. • Coach direct reports on leadership in everyday life. • Support direct reports in developing their functional expertise.
Follow through on performance of leaders	• Give direct reports a fact-based assessment on how well they perform as leaders. • Give direct reports a fact-based assessment on how well they perform on their business objective. • Include feedback on leadership performance in ongoing check-in conversations.
Select leaders	• Select new leaders based on leadership potential – not just functional expertise. • Select direct reports for tomorrow – not just today. • Replace direct reports who consistently fall short of fulfilling their leadership role.

Figure 5.3. Leading a Function: The Job to Be Done.
Source: Copyright Leadership Pipeline Institute.

The group function leader does similar things for the whole enterprise. Enterprise policies and programs are a big part of their role. The group function leaders would usually have some say on the BU function leaders' work, such as establishing the performance standards, approval of the function's strategy and goals, and deployment of talent. The BU function leader must balance what has been decided at group level with the needs of the BU. This adds extra complexity to the function leader role and can lead to conflict with the business leader.

In Figure 5.3 we spell out the responsibilities and some likely actions. Obviously, the actions will vary depending on the current state of the business, the maturity of the organization, and the quality of the staff members.

To elaborate on each category of work in turn: a function leader focuses on the future of the business and of the function they lead.

Function Leaders Help the Business Team Succeed

This responsibility requires complete understanding of the business model, the long-term strategic direction, the goals, and the contributions the other functions will make. This might seem obvious and easy to achieve, but it's not. Mature leaders recognize that they must grasp the larger picture, not just the small piece with which they're comfortable. A function leader can test their readiness for the business team by answering questions such as these:

- What is this business trying to accomplish?

- How does it want to position itself in the market?

- How is the money made in this business?

- What must my function contribute?

- How does my function affect the other functions' ability to contribute?

Function Leaders Develop and Execute Function Strategy

This is a significant shift because up to this leadership level leaders have focused on creating and executing operating plans. In this role, function leaders assess the function's contribution, determining how it should add value. Its strategy may need to be reshaped given changing economic conditions, addition or loss of critical function talent, and available innovation. The function leader needs to have both the vision to see what is needed from the function and the leadership ability to deliver it. Good questions to ask themselves are these:

- How does my function contribute to our competitive advantage now?

- How should my function contribute to competitive advantage in the future?

- What actions should I take to deliver a better competitive advantage now and in the future?

Staying abreast of the state-of-the-art is a challenge for function leaders. Knowing what's possible technically, operationally, and professionally is essential. It directly affects their function's ability to contribute. In our current environment, a strategy that is anything less than state-of-the-art can lead to a competitive disadvantage. In the digital age, information about new technologies is easily acquired, and employees can find and bid for new opportunities electronically. Function leaders need to capitalize on internet searches and create networks to keep informed about new developments. They must also decide if pursuing any new technology is appropriate and worth the time and money.

Function Leaders Drive Function Excellence

This responsibility calls for developing and implementing key function processes. Some processes are implemented across the business such as safety processes, management models, and succession planning. Some processes affect the function customer relationship management processes for sales, and in manufacturing it could be lean processes. The challenge for the function leader is not just identifying and developing the processes. The bigger challenge is often implementing it across the business, in some cases engaging the entire organization and following through year after year. Training is often a big part of this.

The function leader also creates an environment that inspires better ways of working. Function leaders must communicate that innovation is expected throughout the function and not just at the lower or upper levels. Leaders at different levels should give their people room to try new things even if the new things are not successful. Tolerance for mistakes is required for innovation to have a chance. If mistakes are punished no one will try anything new. The tone for all this needs to be set by the function leader.

Function Leaders Build the Function

This responsibility relates both to organization design and having the right capabilities present to meet to meet short-term and long-term business needs.

After getting the function strategy in place, the next step is taking action to add missing capabilities. This is not just about adding people to the function. It may also involve decisions about relocating part of the function to a different geography where more talent is available or outsourcing certain roles while new roles are established. These are often tough people decisions that only the function leader can make.

Enabling the function to deliver on the goals—both operational and strategic—requires an organization structure that allows function-wide initiatives to take hold, the design of the function making sure the right decision can be made by the right people involving the relevant stakeholders. Equally important is to establish a solid function system/rhythm. It is easy as a function to be victimized by events rather than having a solid rhythm for dealing with challenges. The rhythm ensures both strategic and operational things get done in stride. Without a rhythm, in today's fast-paced environment, the function can easily become a victim of circumstances when fixing short-term challenges uses up all the resources.

Function Leaders Take Ownership of Developing Function Talent

In everyday life, all leaders at all levels have talent responsibility but the function leader must set a culture that enables talent to thrive and grow. Talent is not just the few people who may one day have leadership potential or even function leader potential. In today's business environment, specialists are proving to be an even more scarce resource. Consequently, long-term and short-term succession planning relates to both leaders and specialists.

Function Leaders Develop Future Business Leaders

Newly appointed business leaders benefit from having worked in multiple functions during their career. Function leaders should secure cross-function development opportunities. This is one of the true tests of the function leaders. Are they willing to create space for a talented person from another function for a two- or three-year period? That person would have to make an appropriate contribution. If they can, they will demonstrate the adaptability, breadth, and learning ability needed for business leader roles. From a short-term function perspective, it would seem better to dedicate all key roles to function experts. This is not the talent development thinking we expect from a function leader.

Function Leaders Follow Through on the Performance of Leaders

Results must be delivered for the business to succeed. Operating results, financial results, technical results, and leadership results are tracked and measured. Frequently there is a missing ingredient that happens to be the most important one—leadership results:

setting a clear direction, getting buy-in, assigning appropriate goals and tasks, tracking progress, developing their own people, and preparing some for larger roles are critical parts of the job. Performance on these leadership responsibilities must be thoroughly monitored and measured. Frequent and short progress discussions help keep performance on track.

Function Leaders (Select Leaders-of-Leaders)

Leaders-of-leaders are usually familiar with choosing leaders-of-others. As function leaders they will be selecting leaders-of-leaders. The selection criteria are different and the observations required aren't straightforward. The two most important criteria to consider are (1) have they fully transitioned to their leader-of-others role and (2) are they able to grasp the workings of the whole function, not just their assigned portion? The two next steps are (1) asking the manage-self population (specialists, technicians, analysts, etc.) about their development plan and the coaching they receive and (2) asking candidates their opinion on function issues.

The Transition to the Role

This transition is tougher than it seems. On the surface the differences between a leader-of-leaders role and a function leader role appear negligible. A number of significant challenges lurk below the surface. New function leaders usually get little support, if any, from their business leader when stepping into this role. Function peers on the business team will start demanding things from the newly appointed function leader on day one. Those demands will only increase. The honeymoon period at this level of the organization is very short and is often limited to the very first business team meeting. After that, reality sets in.

A good start in the function leader role can be achieved by being highly skilled functionally, having good leadership skills, and becoming well-liked by the function peers. The time and energy

Leading Leaders

WORK VALUES

- Achieving results through leaders
- Success in value chain
- Ambiguity
- Values based leadership

TIME APPLICATION

- Long-term (two to three years) business planning
- Resource allocation
- Providing input upwards for strategy planning
- Managing boundaries between teams
- Managing boundaries to peer organizations

SKILLS

- Organizational design
- Selecting leaders
- Managing stakeholders
- Coaching of leaders
- Assessing performance of leaders
- Building a diverse organization
- Building agility within the organization
- Strategic capability building

Leading a Function

WORK VALUES

- Valuing what you don't know
- Competitive advantage
- Total business results
- Being a member of the business team
- Multifunctional thinking

TIME APPLICATION

- Preparing for and participating in business team meetings
- Seeking external benchmark and inspiration
- Spending time with functional talent
- Building a strong function

SKILLS

- Function strategy development
- Design function structure
- Function talent management
- Function KPIs
- Creating function system/rhythm
- Managing function budget
- Creating work climate that supports innovation

Figure 5.4. Leader-of-Leaders Versus Function Leaders Core Differences in Work Values, Time Application, and Skills.
Source: Copyright Leadership Pipeline Institute.

required to build relations sometimes holds function leaders back from investing time and energy for executing the necessary transition. Figure 5.4 offers an overview of the necessary transition in work values, time application, and skills for function leaders. In some organizations adding to these may be required, depending on the challenges. For enterprise function leaders in organizations with multiple businesses structure enterprise policy, programs, and standards should be added.

What were the two or three main challenges you faced during the first three to six months after moving into your function leader role?	What two or three things do you miss most about only leading a practice area within the function or part of the function rather than being a function leader?	What two or three things would you like to spend more time on in your current position, but seem unable to find time for?	What are the two or three most important skills you have come to realize you need as a function leader?
1. No one defining my agenda or business objectives. Everything has to come from myself 2. Reporting to a person who does not really understand my function 3. Having several functional practice areas reporting to me about which I have no experience 4. Building credibility/ trust among functional peers	1. Having a more defined role in terms of business deliverables 2. Not anything significant	1. Time outside the company gathering external inspiration 2. Getting to better understand peer functions 3. Strategic work both in relation to the function and the business 4. Strategic alignment with peer functions	1. Defining and driving functional KPIs across the organization 2. Building functional competitive edge 3. Understanding business strategy 4. Understanding peer functions 5. Organizational design

Figure 5.5. Consolidated Results for Function Leaders.
Source: Copyright Leadership Pipeline Institute.

Figure 5.4 illustrates the transition from leading leaders to leading a function. In smaller functions, leaders will move directly from a leader-of-others role to the leader-of-function role. There is nothing wrong with that, but it does make the transition even more challenging.

In Chapter 2 we described the action research since 2010. In Figure 5.5 you see the consolidated results for function leaders.

Work Values

Enterprise function leaders must represent the enterprise as well as their functions. That means thinking and evaluating like a CEO relative to their function. The policies and programs they produce must reflect enterprise needs. It starts with adopting a total enterprise mindset.

Function leaders in a business need a business mindset. When effective function leaders in a business enter a business meeting, they do not fight for their function. They fight for the business. They may have conflicting priorities with other functions and battle with other functions over the budgets. If they always try to get more than their fair share for their function, they will create pipeline blockages by instilling a partisan mentality that is at odds with business success. Individuals who are promoted to this level must shift away from a function value system and to one that is business or enterprise focused.

Because function leaders have to deal with so many new variables and unfamiliar issues, the challenge is twofold:

- Learning to manage what's new

- Learning to value new information and ideas

Valuing what's new and unfamiliar is a particular challenge for less mature function leaders. By *mature*, we are not referring to their age; we are referring to their self-esteem and their self-confidence and most of all their ability to manage their emotions. The ability to delay gratification until others have succeeded is a key indicator of maturity. The less mature function leaders often fall into the trap of having to know all the answers, feeling they must justify their promotion. They're resolutely unwilling to ask questions or say "I don't know" for fear of being thought undeserving of their leadership status. They are starting to fail and will clog the pipeline.

Ideally, function leaders love to learn what they don't know. Their subordinates will accept questions and uncertainties early in the new function leader's tenure and are eager to fill them in. Customers and end users, too, will be more than willing to provide knowledge and ideas. The key is for function leaders to engage others in dialogue, listen carefully, and reflect on what they're told. Function leaders truly value their work only when they truly understand it, and an eagerness to learn will help them adjust their work values appropriately.

Effective function leaders start by spending time in areas that are new to them, appreciating input from peers and external networks, and reaching out to people rather than waiting for them to come forward.

Function leaders are members of a multifunction team so multifunction thinking is essential. The vast majority of function leaders have worked only in their current function. Although they are not completely ignorant of the work done in the other functions, they are not knowledgeable enough in most instances to be true partners. Knowledge of the results, plans, competitive edge, and methods of the other functions makes it possible to develop a multifunction thought process. Function leaders who make the best decisions and achieve the most ambitious goals are those who take the impact on the other functions into account. Success of the business, not just the function, is the goal. Applying a multifunction thought process enables the high level of integration required for business success.

Underpinning an effective transition is the development of the right mindset. Up to this point leaders have needed an operational mindset. Getting things done in the best way has been primary. Now a strategic mindset is required. They must answer questions such as "How do our competitors do this?" "What could we do to get ahead of them?" "Where is technology going and what of that can I use?" Thinking outside the business and bringing that thinking in is new and challenging.

Time Application

It's important that function leaders spend time in a few new, significant areas:

- Preparing for and participating in business team meetings

- Seeking external benchmarks

- Understanding the state-of-the-art and strengths of competitors for function strategy purposes

- Building function talent, particularly the leaders

Unfortunately, column three in Figure 5.5 shows that function leaders in general feel they spend too little time doing the following:

- Gathering external inspiration outside the company

- Learning more about peer functions

- Working on strategy, both in relation to the function and the business

- Developing strategic alignment with peer functions

We worked with a CIO on designing a framework for developing IT specialist talent within his function. During lunch one day, he shared that after four years in the role he had been moved from the CIO role to a new IT project and operations role that would report to the CIO taking over his job. The reason given by the business leader was that "she recognized that the IT function received good internal scores on the cross-function service satisfaction survey and all projects were executed on time and within budget, but the function wasn't coming up with breakthroughs that could strengthen the business's position. She felt that all new ideas on how IT could support the business had come from the other functions."

At this stage, he was very disappointed about both the demotion and the reason for it. As he pointed out, "Fine, they want me to spend time on the strategic part of the function agenda, but whenever we have a business meeting all they talk about are operational IT issues, and the last time I had a one-on-one conversation with the business leader she spent 10 minutes discussing why her email application was working slower than usual on her phone."

He is not alone. We have found that many function leaders don't feel they are viewed as a true business partner—by their business leader or by their peers—at least not until it is too late. It would seem logical for the business leader to give specific guidance, but we don't see enough evidence that they do. New function leaders must spend time working through this problem.

Skills

Acquiring the necessary new skills for new function leaders is complex because now they must think outside the function and business. Other functions in their business need to be aligned in many cases for function programs to work. The skills needed at this level are not skills that everyone can simply learn. We see function leaders struggling in all different areas and many in multiple areas. A couple of examples can illustrate this.

Case study

We were staying at an upscale hotel in a major city. The check-in line was out the door, which was unusual for a Friday night. Much grumbling and complaining could be heard. There was only one person handling check-ins. The next day we asked the check-in person what the problem had been. She said Friday nights are usually slow, so the marketing department (which was located in a different city) was trying to boost revenue and raise the hotel's profile. They had launched a "Sweet Hart's Weekend" promotion to attract locals who don't usually use the hotel. Two nights and two breakfasts were offered at a bargain price for Friday and Saturday when revenue was always low. The marketing plan worked, and revenue tripled—but the long-term outcome was poor. The guest survey results were terrible: the hour-long check-in line killed guests' enthusiasm, and their mood was further tested by Saturday's equally long breakfast line. This happened because marketing never told the operations function about the program, so the required staff members weren't in place and there wasn't enough bacon. We later had a discussion with a senior officer at the hotel's headquarters; we discovered the marketing function had a KPI to increase revenue by 10%, and operations had a KPI of reducing operating costs by 5%.

Why weren't the right function KPIs in place, accepted, and understood by all functions? After all, function leaders have been setting objectives throughout their careers. The answer: function KPIs should be communicated to an entire organization because they frequently affect everyone. (For example, measurements on safety, retention, quality, diversity, client retention, and engagement apply to everyone.) As the hotel example shows, KPIs can easily end up driving conflicting behavior if they are not carefully thought through and integrated with other functions.

It may make perfectly good sense to define a retention KPI such as "less than 5% turnover on high performers." However, doing it requires cross-company alignment on judging performance. If it is defined as a performance score of four on a five scale, but you don't have a credible performance review process in which performance scores are aligned across functions, you cannot be sure that this will support business results. It is easy to retain high performers by paying them more than market. Accordingly, if the retention KPI does not go hand in hand with a well-managed compensation plan, we may meet the KPI of less than 5% turnover on high performers, but do so at an acceptable cost.

Function leaders through their actions create the work climate that supports innovation. These actions can include making sure that frontline leaders develop psychological safety within their teams, provide sufficient budget for trying new things, develop a tolerance for some mistakes, and personally support their people's efforts. Setting the parameters for innovation through the function strategy is also a key requirement. Perhaps the most powerful ingredients are requiring all staff members to improve what they do, not just repeat what they did yesterday.

Creating a work climate that supports innovation is not just a single string discipline. It requires thorough knowledge of human behavior, innovation processes, psychological safety, and function strategy. Performance management, reward programs, and budget planning are also needed.

As you can appreciate, setting meaningful function KPIs requires that everything supporting these KPIs is also in place. Function manager success requires strong relationships with peers, integration of plans, and acceptance of a common purpose. The complication in these relationships comes from conflicting goals such as we saw in the hotel example. Complication also comes from old grievances, such as "Why don't you sell what we make?" and "No, why don't you make what we can sell!"

Strategic thinking is an important new skill. There is no guarantee the new function leader will master it. At lower levels in the function, they were doing operational planning. Operational planning starts inside the organization and looks at what is working and what isn't. Reaching outside the organization to find improvements is frequently done. Strategic thinking starts outside the organization and looks for ways to improve, innovate, expand, or grow, usually by looking at least three years out. Processing large amounts of data, assessing competitors, thinking about possibilities, looking for ways to create an advantage are basic requirements. Strategic thinking and planning are a big step up for new function leaders.

Typical Transition Issues

Similar to leaders at lower levels, it is easy for function leaders to rely on the same work values, time application, and skills that they relied on in their previous positions. This is a clear warning sign that they are not handling this transition properly, and it's often masked by their high degree of competence in a specific sub-function work. They look as though they're doing a terrific job because they continue to come up with great ideas and generate results, mostly in one area. But they haven't embraced what really counts in this leadership role. Function leaders who have not made this transition successfully don't move the business toward strategic goals or competitive advantage. If they favor one part of their organization, they can create anger, resentment, and

Typical Transition Issues

- Struggling to balance the dual relationship with both the business leader and the group function head
- Failing to integrate own function agenda with peer function agendas
- Prioritizing well-known areas over unfamiliar areas
- Continuing doing operational work rather than strategic work
- Preserving the status quo

Figure 5.6. Typical Transition Issues for Function Leaders.
Source: Copyright Leadership Pipeline Institute.

turnover in other parts. They end up hurting the function's performance in the long run. Let's review the typical transition challenges using some examples. (See Figure 5.6.)

Struggling to Balance Their Relationship with Both the Business Leader and the Group Function Head

Function leaders in a business may end up serving two masters. One master is the business leader they report to and the other is the group function leader. While managing these two masters you also need to maintain strong relationships with BU peer function leaders and the different centers of excellence within the group functions.

Case study

Jane is a BU human resource function leader for the consumer banking arm of a large global bank. Jane is astute about balancing her many points of contact.

(continued)

The bank recently selected a new head of group HR from outside the bank. The CEO gave a mandate to reinvent how the group HR function adds value to the enterprise. This led to a redefined talent process, implementation of key psychometric assessment tools, redesign of the succession planning process, and a new internal cross-business talent mobility strategy. When group HR started to impose these new standards on the consumer bank, the head of group HR and the business leader of the consumer bank "bumped heads," because the consumer bank historically had been the most successful BU within the company on people issues and had thus operated with relative autonomy in the past.

Jane was placed in a difficult position. Others might well have chosen sides and played politics. Still, other people might have tried to avoid the conflict altogether. Jane, however, was operating at the right leadership level and recognized that she needed to keep her points of contact in balance. To that end, Jane implemented the new succession planning process as it was easy to work with and it did not jeopardize all the work on succession planning already done in the consumer bank. She also created a plan for implementing the test tools, but over a longer period of time, and without testing existing employees. She agreed with the head of group HR that maybe the existing talent process in the consumer bank could benefit from some minor adjustments from the group talent process. She left the cross-business mobility strategy for her business leader to discuss further with his peers in the other businesses as this was something that had to be implemented in concert across the company.

This position satisfied the new group HR leader. At the same time, however, she protected the consumer bank from what she considered unreasonable group HR requests. That position pleased her business leader and her function peers within the BU.

Certainly, there were other situations involving these two leaders that put demands on Jane to balance complex conflicts.

For instance, when the consumer bank adjusted its strategy six months later and immediately needed more people, the management team in the consumer bank just started poaching people from the other BUs without following the group HR process of posting the jobs and achieving transparency in the selection process. Of course, Jane quickly got calls from the head of group HR and peer HR function leaders in the other BUs.

Jane was able also to build a bridge with HR peers because of her competence and her insistence on finding common ground.

Failing to Integrate Own Function Agenda with Peer Function Agendas

When function leaders fail to perform at the level that's required, it's often because of their deceptively successful performance. In other words, they excel at leading the function in one area and this performance obscures their deficits in other key result areas—obscures them temporarily, that is, until negative consequences eventually emerge.

Case study

BRC is a business that makes coloring additives for a variety of applications. The enterprise comprised six businesses and BRC was the smallest. In general, the marketing function was weak across the enterprise. BRC had grown fast over its first few years because of great applications sold to a narrow group of customers. But its growth had stalled. New customers were needed to help fix the problem. For this purpose, they brought in Aiyana as vice president of marketing, and she seemed like an ideal hire. Previously, she had been the marketing func-

(continued)

tion leader at two businesses about the same size as BRC, though, they were part of much smaller enterprises.

Aiyana inherited a number of challenges, including a small staff of widely varying abilities, a lack of enterprise expertise in marketing work, and an absence of a defined role and space for the marketing function on the business team. In terms of this last challenge, Aiyana's predecessor was an order taker and had not carved out much time for the function at business team meetings or gained much respect from peers. Fortunately for Aiyana, her reputation preceded her, and her peers and the marketing team greeted her enthusiastically. Aiyana's function results were strong for the first year and even stronger for the second. Excellent strategic analysis and market planning helped her identify and open new markets. She coached the team and they became more skillful at market and customer analysis, customer engagement, and selling. She added a talented market development person who had instant access to new client pools. Because of her acumen, Aiyana helped the company achieve double-digit sales growth in her first two years.

Her success was obvious, but her record was not without blemish. Some of her peers began to complain to the business leader about her: Aiyana did not involve them in her thinking and planning, operations was racing to keep up; quality was slipping, finance did not feel that it had time for credit checks on new customers, human resources was concerned that two of Aiyana's marketing stars had fared poorly in interviews for leadership positions and were only selected for their professional capabilities, customers began complaining about errors on their bills and declining product quality. By the middle of the third year, Aiyana had become isolated from her peers. Sales growth was still good, but the profit growth was only half the rate of sales growth.

As skilled as Aiyana was at building sales, she fell short in other parts of the job:

- Aiyana drove sales growth without regard for the capability of the other functions, particularly operations, to respond. She did not seek her peers' views on how much sales growth the business could handle; she never bothered to learn what the other functions could do, what their plans were, and what challenges they faced.

- Aiyana focused her team's coaching and development on professional skills to the exclusion of helping them develop leadership skills. As a result, her people were not promotable, and they did not deliver on their required leadership performance.

- Aiyana made assumptions about how the finance function worked based on her experience in other companies. BRC's finance function had much more rigorous risk management procedures and took the time to do more credit checks, set up automated processing, and adjust forecasts based on changes in ordering patterns. They were more sophisticated and needed better communication from Aiyana. The finance officer tried to schedule meetings with her, but in vain.

Prioritizing Well-Known Areas over Unfamiliar Areas

Case study

Asahi had spent his entire career within the manufacturing and supply chain functions. In most ways, Asahi excelled as a leader-of-leaders. He empowered direct reports to test innovative production technology and coached them on how to

(continued)

develop their people. Though Asahi was generally satisfied with how things were going, he did grumble about not receiving sufficient project money to accelerate the production area's growth. During Asahi's two-year tenure, his operation doubled in size and he and his team were rewarded for their contributions. The best reward came when Asahi was named as the manufacturing function leader.

Asahi had eight leaders-of-leaders in total. Those reporting directly were responsible for production planning, quality control, purchasing, manufacturing, engineering, and production. In addition, information technology, human resources, and other support units reported to Asahi on a dotted line. Most of these people were older than Asahi because he had advanced quickly.

As a function leader, Asahi made an effort to gain knowledge about purchasing and two production operations, areas where he had little or no previous exposure. He toured these areas and reviewed their goals, plans, and budgets. After what he felt was an objective analysis, Asahi concluded that purchasing wasn't well run and that the two production operations were overstaffed. He concluded that if he shifted some money that was going to these areas to projects in his former new product production area, the manufacturing group would be well served.

After Asahi cut their budgets, the direct reports responsible for these areas were incensed. When Asahi told them about his observed inefficiencies, the purchasing head resigned then and there. When Asahi's boss was informed of what had taken place, he was even more upset than the direct reports.

Asahi's surface analysis didn't reveal that the two production operations played a critical role in maintaining strong customer relationships; it also didn't reveal that purchasing had been working long and hard to replace vendors whose quality was slipping and that the purchasing head was highly skilled at finding and establishing relationships with the best quality suppliers. He also built a strong network throughout the business. Asahi had jumped to conclusions based on his limited knowledge and expertise and had used his findings as an excuse to fund his long-standing pet projects.

Playing favorites in this way is a sign that someone is having difficulty with this role. Typically, new function leaders are asked to supervise important areas in which they have little or no experience. Without a good frame of reference, they may react by overvaluing their former, well-known area of responsibility and undervaluing the unknown. Asahi needed to transition from an operational orientation focused on a few projects to a strategic orientation focused on all the function's projects. Unfortunately, no one told Asahi about this need or developed him in this direction.

As part of our leadership diagnostics work, we usually use a simple time application exercise to reveal whether a function leader is on track. New function leaders may want to use it for testing themselves.

- How much time, specifically, are you spending with the different units reporting to you?

- Is your time distribution between the different units justified by current critical issues, for example, less experienced leader of the unit, or is it simply that these were the units where you had worked?

Continuing Doing Operational Work Rather Than Strategic Work

Spending hours and hours solving problems their team brings to them may seem important. It is actually a sign that the new function manager is still doing their old job. Long lines of people at their door makes them feel important but actually means they haven't delegated properly. Coming forward with a shallow strategy means they aren't spending enough time on strategy. Not being available for meetings with their peers means they haven't accepted the responsibility for building those relationships. When the agendas for their staff meetings are focused on today and yesterday, not on tomorrow, it is a strong sign they are stuck in the present. Strategy is built by looking outward and forward. There are a considerable number of indicators that someone is focusing on operating work, not strategic work. The balance may be tipped toward operating matters early in the new assignment while there is learning needed. When it persists long after starting the position that function manager is stuck and needs help to become successful.

Preserving the Status Quo

Preserving the status quo is usually a result of someone who lacks the self-confidence and maturity to address the more daunting aspects of the leadership role. They fear the challenges associated with continuously reinventing the function's role, upgrading the talent, canceling initiatives that will never make a real difference to the business, and pursuing bold initiatives even though the chance of success is uncertain.

This role requires a person who has the courage for "finding the necessary bold move I need to make but I am not making right now." They should proactively invite other functions to challenge them, and they should have the courage to challenge other functions and raise their voice in business strategy discussions. However, we see function leaders who are highly compensated but behave merely as a steward of the function. They were seduced by the glamour of the job when it was offered, but the day after taking it they were simply overwhelmed by the real job to be done.

When function leaders are not viewed as equals by their function peers, it affects the entire function's ability to create results. We have observed many function leaders who became so involved in politics, operational transactions, board of director commit-tees, and the like that they don't have much time to think about where the function should be headed. They also don't devote much time to considering the function's current state or ensuring the function makes an appropriate contribution. All in all, they lose touch with the function state-of-the-art and spend their time preserving the status quo. They become reluctant to change and are risk averse.

The risk-averse function leader will usually lack the ability to make trade-offs properly within the function. People in the busi-ness don't always notice when there are activities that were stopped. They only notice years later what should have been done but wasn't. Consequently, it becomes a safe bet for the risk-averse function leader just to maintain what is already taking place, rather than prioritizing hard decisions and closing down activities that are not supporting business strategy, profitability, and competitive advantage, or starting up activities that support the same.

An Important Outcome

Maturity is a result of learning from success and from mistakes—in other words, learning from experience. Ideally, people will have had the opportunity to see the business broadly and become immersed in diverse situations where they succeed and where they err. They will have had the occasions to exhibit immature behavior and learn from their mistakes through mentoring, coaching, feedback, and so on. Given that many relatively young, high-performing people are being promoted to function leader positions, the odds are that this maturity hasn't fully developed. To help these leaders grow, place them on task forces, teams, and committees of leaders from different functions or sub-functions with different backgrounds, skills, and experi-ence. Having to work effectively with people who are different is a growth experience. Not only will function leaders learn about new areas of work but also they will establish relationships with new people who use different methods and skills. It will take them out of the cocoon of the familiar function and help them see a wider range of choice.

Developing strategic competencies can be a more formal process. After three to six months on the job, training in these skills can be done through university classes, consultants, or in-house resources. The best method of training, however, involves hands-on learning activities in which the leader uses the function's own data, challenges, and resources in a strategy-related assignment. After completing the assignment, the leader should be evaluated and receive feedback.

Development aimed at helping people become whole as function leaders can involve a variety of activities. One of the best is meeting with other function leaders who can share their assessment of this specific leader's function. Where do they see a need for improvement? Where do they see opportunities for synergy? The perspectives of peers can provide a new function leader with an appreciation of their function that is much more wide-ranging than they would ordinarily possess.

Development progress can be measured by using a calendar check. Function leaders have to make significant shifts in how they spend their time if they're going to transition to this new leadership level successfully. Time has to be blocked out for strategy sessions, communication meetings with a variety of sub-function representatives, and so on. Function leaders should note on their calendars the time they've devoted to these activities. In addition, they should be spending time benchmarking cross-industry and be involved in local learning networks. A regular review of their calendars will tell whether they're really devoting the time necessary to develop as function leaders.

Perhaps the best way to measure developmental progress, however, is to watch for signs of maturity. We've noted many likely signs. But maturity can also be measured in development of traits such as humility. Mature leaders know they don't have to be the expert in every area of the function (and in fact, can't be), and are willing to admit that others know more than they do and are willing to learn from them. Similarly, mature leaders recognize that if they're going to succeed, they need to get cooperation from others. To do so, they'll delegate, communicate, and ensure that information flows smoothly and quickly.

Finally, a clear sign of maturity is letting go of old silo behaviors. When silos were the rule, functions and sub-functions worked apart rather than together. Although management may attempt to tear down these silos, the old attitudes might persist. Mature leaders will turn away from a narrow dedication to their function and embrace a more integrated, total business philosophy.

6

Leading a Business

There is no denying the shock leaders feel when they take their first business leader position and begin to realize all that is involved. Everything about this job is different from any other role and we have seen that it is the most dramatic and most difficult role transition. The transition has to be managed carefully. There is significantly more at stake, both good and bad. It is done with the whole organization and many outside groups watching, and the runway is much shorter. Despite all that most business leaders say it is the best job they ever had.

The center of this role is to produce short-term and long-term profit while strengthening the organization and without exhausting all the resources. A whole new thought process is required. Despite the dramatic change required, the vast majority of business leaders love this job. They typically have responsibility for both production (cost) and sales (revenue). Because they have these major pieces there is an enhanced control of the business's outcomes. Incumbents are highly visible to a wide audience in the business and externally so there isn't any place to practice. Nonetheless, the position is much sought-after.

Function leaders produce products or services or support that satisfy customers and create a competitive advantage for the business. Their compelling questions begin with "Can we . . . ?" Can we make it? Can we sell it? Can we attract the talent we want? Can we lower our costs without spoiling the product or service? Can we adopt the new technology? Can we be fast to market? Can we complete this deal? These are important and fundamental questions that should be answered. When the answer is yes the business leader steps in.

Business leaders are responsible for ensuring the business will make profit in both the short and long term while making the organization stronger and using resources wisely. They must learn to ask different questions focused primarily on "should we or shouldn't we." Will we make any profit if we do it? Will we have to change our business model? Will other important programs in other areas suffer? Will we get an appropriate return on our investment? Will we have to do it for every customer or supplier or employee? Is this the best thing to do for the long term? Just because we can do something it doesn't mean we should. The business manager decides.

The Heft and Scope of the Role

To avoid confusion about who is a business leader, we offer the following definition, which is useful in most companies. Quite simply the business leader is accountable for profit and has decision-making authority for cost and revenue. Furthermore, they have function leaders reporting to them either directly or with dotted lines. Managing the trade-offs between cost and revenue is especially critical. So, having only one or the other disqualifies an individual from being a true business leader. People running product lines are often called business leader but they usually have either cost or revenue authority. Their authority usually concerns products and related matters, not usually production and sales. People who run large production or sales organizations might also be called business leaders but they only control one of the two key variables for the business.

Finding the right starting point for succeeding at the business leader layer isn't easy. If the mental picture is "hitting my profit targets," suboptimal decisions are likely. Longer-term needs may be ignored for the sake of short-term profit. Important support activities will be ignored. Investment might be inadequate. The most appropriate mindset is "building a money-making machine." It will help business leaders understand that everything counts and they need help from their team.

A challenging and perhaps confusing aspect of the business leader's position is that they may also be the enterprise leader, sometimes called the chief executive officer (CEO). Job requirements probably double if that is the case. Investors, shareholders, governments, communities, and other special interest groups require their attention. Usually, there is very little guidance on how to perform the role. For very small companies the enterprise leader's time requirements are usually small. As businesses grow their visibility increases and enterprise leader's duties become a major time-eater. In this chapter we will focus primarily on the business leader role. We will discuss the enterprise leader role in detail in Chapter 7.

The Job to Be Done

To elaborate on each category of work in turn: business leaders build the organization while delivering short-term and long-term profit. (See Figure 6.1.)

Business Leaders Deliver Short-Term and Long-Term Profit

It is easy to think of the business leader's profit responsibility in terms of numbers: the financials. Looking at the work that way can lead to numbers-based decisions, for example, "cut costs quickly," "get rid of training," "pump up sales by giving discounts." This may be slightly exaggerated but not by much. The impact of these

The Work	Required Activities
Profit—short and long term	• Market relevant value proposition. • Manage revenue and cost, drive efficiency. • Balance short- and long-term initiatives.
Business strategy	• Competitive analysis, identify threats. • Identify opportunities, new market positions, new technology. • Enable innovation and growth.
Organization alignment	• Free flow of information downward and upward. • Distribution of accountability and authority to lowest level. • All functions aligned with strategy.
Business leadership	• Personally connect with all levels. • Establish common purpose and get by-in. • Select and build strong business team.
External presence	• Community engagement and events. • Customer connection and retention. • Industry participation and presence.
Talent management	• Succession planning at all levels. • Develop direct reports, set standards. • Leadership development programs for all leaders.

Figure 6.1. Leading a Business: The Job to Be Done.
Source: Copyright Leadership Pipeline Institute.

quick, numbers-based decisions can be crippling in the longer term. Laying off valuable people, giving discounts that aren't sustainable, and future leaders not getting needed preparation can all compromise the business. The most important skill for a business leader is learning how to build a machine that generates a profit now and will do so in the future. Time must be taken to study the organization and learn precisely how money is made and how things are done in all parts of the business. Using digitization to improve the business is easier when the business leader knows exactly how the business works and where improvement is needed. Determining who exactly is contributing to getting products and services made and delivered to the customer on time at the right cost and quality is fundamental to good business decision-making. Valuing every step and every person is part of this job. Many of these steps and the people involved might not have been as valued in the previous function job. Using digitization for business improvement, not just functional improvement, is a basic skill requirement.

Business Leaders Develop Business Strategy

The antidote for pursuing profit as numbers with the problems that engenders is having a bigger picture of where the business should be headed. This bigger picture is developed through strategic planning. The main purpose for a strategy is defining where to position the business in its industry and in the world around it. Examination of competitors, economic trends, state-of-the-art technology, and talent availability are required. Positioning ideas such as becoming global by entering additional countries, being the market leader in innovation or customer service, being the low-cost provider are common. The strategy guides business decision-making, investment decisions in particular.

Business leaders need to develop strategic thinking skills and have the courage to pick a direction. Encouraging active participation by all the business team members is the only way to get all the needed information and analysis.

Case study

A health-care delivery company we worked with wanted to pursue a rapid expansion in the geography it served. They had built a strong reputation for quality and service in its local market. The business development leader proposed an expansion plan that had the whole business team and the business leader in particular very excited. It was clear from

> the analysis that most of the country would be interested. The human resources leader asked for a day to do some research. She reported to the business team the next day. The proposed growth would require hiring every graduating nursing student for the next four years. A much more modest growth was then adopted.

Business Leaders Use Digitization to Achieve Organization Alignment

In order to create and maintain alignment in an organization it is essential to use digitization effectively. Digitization offers many helpful options for tracking progress, improving decision-making, reducing costs, innovating, communicating quickly with a wide audience, and many others. An ever-increasing bundle of systems and tools makes data of all kinds available quickly. Deciding what data is useful and what isn't necessary are part of the job. Business leaders make the final decisions on automation and artificial intelligence, what communication vehicles should be used, and which equipment to buy. Striking the balance between automation and customer satisfaction is critical. Customers sooner or later want to talk to a human being. How to strike the balance among speed, efficiency, and customers' need for human support is an ongoing challenge. Any use of technology should improve the value proposition for customers, investors, and the business itself. The function leaders need to actively recommend what to do.

Data availability at lower levels has enabled businesses to make pricing changes based on instantaneous available data on traffic or volume. There is little or no direct impact on cost but revenue is affected. Information technology specialists create systems that cut across the business and enable others to make better decisions. The business leader ultimately decides what technology to use, what not to use, and when to do either.

Although digitization affects everyone, business leaders carry the heaviest load. They make the final decision on what to buy, develop, and use. There are consequences to these decisions:

- If the technology used is not up-to-date, it will be difficult to attract and retain talent. Tracking this closely and making necessary changes will be critical.

- Every function will want something but the business won't be able to afford it all. Hard choices have to be made and some will feel slighted. Sound logic is required to gain acceptance and cooperation from the business team in making the trade-offs.

- Employees have more power because they have more information, better tools, and many job opportunities. They want to use that power. Flexibility about career paths, organization structure, job design, and their role in decision-making is required.

- Decisions made, or not made, will be criticized and probably publicized in social media. A well-thought-out communication strategy can win followers and avoid trouble.

- Customer expectations will only increase. Keeping up so expectations can be managed and customers retained is a never-ending challenge.

- Some choices in systems won't work out. Living with mistakes can't go on for very long.

Digitization and the related technology are a blessing and a curse depending on how well business leaders learn to use it and how much its power is valued. Although the functions may fall in love with the technology, the business manager values its impact on the business's value proposition.

Business Leaders Are Role Models for All Leaders

Every leadership position has some degree of visibility; everyone has a boss who is watching them to see how they perform. The visibility at this level, however, is much more intense and comes from every direction. Especially from below. Everyone in the business has a great deal riding on how well the new business leader can run the business. Investors want to know if the returns will meet their expectations. The local community wants to know if jobs will continue. Customers and suppliers want to know if the relationship will last. Although function leaders receive a good deal of scrutiny most of it comes from inside the business. The business leader bears the brunt of scrutiny from a much wider audience.

Business leaders possess great power over projects, plans, and people and this power makes their every move subject to scrutiny. Just about everyone watching has questions:

- Will this leader make it?

- Will the strategy change?

- Will the top team be kept in place?

- Will their former function be favored?

- Will my project continue or be killed?

- Will they change now that they have the power?

- What will happen to the culture?

- Will the right investments be made?

- Can we renegotiate contracts fairly?

There are many more questions. The new business leader must learn to anticipate questions and value them as opportunities to get important messages communicated. The skill of thoughtful response to challenging questions, both formal and informal, is an inevitable requirement for success.

Business Leaders Shape the Company's External Presence

As mentioned, many outsiders have a personal intertest in the success of business leaders. Customers, suppliers, competitors, communities, and governments all want to know what the business becomes under this leader. It affects all of them if the business succeeds, changes direction, or fails. Interest in strategies, growth initiatives, accessibility, and likely support are topics they want to hear about. An organized approach to communication, engagement, and support has to be conveyed by the business leader.

Active engagement in addressing social issues has been an increasing requirement. Establishing the business as a "good citizen" enables a smooth external path to an appropriate external presence. Mishandling this subject gets communicated to the world instantly and produces forceful backlash. Business results can be adversely affected in a matter of hours. External communications have to be carefully planned and delivered with conviction.

Active engagement with customers, industry groups, community organizations, governments in some cases, and special-interest groups is part of the job to be done. Promoting the business and listening for useful information are reasons.

Business Leaders Set the Tone for Talent Management

Successful business leaders we have worked with do something many less successful ones don't: they set the tone for talent management. Through personal involvement and program requirements they build strong succession planning processes, leadership development programs, and recruiting and coaching, and they make it clear that this work is highly valued and should be given top priority.

The Transition to the Role

Some business leaders move into the role from a function leader role. Others move from a leader-of-leaders role or a leader-of-others role. Although several routes are possible the underlying challenge is moving from function work to business work.

Thinking differently as we just explained is an important part of the transition to business leader. There are several other important changes. To be successful, enabling full performance from all functions is required. In most cases the new business leader has worked only in one or two of them. The experienced ones are valued more highly. Valuing all functions equally is the only way to get full performance from all.

Day-to-day problem-solving is important in function work. Business leaders have to give that up. Seeing the patterns of problems and their root cause is important to the business leader. Everyone else in the business is responsible, in one way or another, for solving them. The business leader makes systemic changes to keep problems from recurring.

Function leaders spend time learning the state-of-the-art. Business leaders learn the state of business. What's new in products, strategies, markets, legislation, and so on is important information for setting direction and making decisions.

Integrating the function leaders into a business team takes time and effort. Establishing common purpose, balancing resource allocation, providing equal opportunities for input, and holding regular meetings are required. (See Figure 6.2.)

In Chapter 1 we described the applied research we have carried since 2010. In Figure 6.3, you see the consolidated results for the business leaders.

Work Values

As leaders step out of their traditional functional role and step up to leading a full spectrum of functions, they need to take time to learn about the key ingredients of all functions and how they fit together to produce results. On the surface this isn't difficult, but it takes time, intelligence, and perseverance. What becomes difficult is learning to value all functions appropriately. Several years of working in one function will make that function important and well understood. From this leadership point on, functional

Leading a Business

WORK VALUES
- Pursuit of short-term and long-term profit
- Creating shareholder/stakeholder value
- Perpetuating the business and the company
- Building the organization

TIME APPLICATION
- Succession planning and talent management
- Preparing for and running board and business team meetings
- Developing strategy
- External involvement: customers, community, industry

SKILLS
- Building and executing business strategy
- Designing and delivering the business model
- Integrating functions
- Creating business system/rhythm
- Managing complexity
- Communicating to broad and diverse audiences
- Selecting and using data

Figure 6.2. Leading a Business: Required Work Values, Time Application, and Skills.
Source: Copyright Leadership Pipeline Institute.

What were the two or three main challenges you faced during the first three to six months after moving into your business leader role?	What two or three things do you miss most about leading a function rather than leading the entire business?	What two or three things would you like to spend more time on in your current position, but seem unable to find time for?	What are the two or three most important skills you have come to realize you need as a business leader?
1. Setting the right business team 2. Patience; allowing the functions time to execute on decisions made 3. Appreciating that there are many things within different functions that I have yet to learn about	1. Having close peers 2. Being much less in frequent dialogue with my direct manager 3. Not anything significant	1. Meeting informally with customers 2. Having "me time" where I am not in meetings 3. Seeking external inspiration	1. Managing priority conflicts between functions 2. Mobilizing the entire organization (much more challenging than mobilizing a function) 3. Building a management team out of highly capable, dominant, and ambitious direct reports

Figure 6.3. Consolidated Applied Research Results for Business Leaders.
Source: Copyright Leadership Pipeline Institute.

prejudice becomes a serious problem. It can result in everything from overreliance on one function to failing to maximize the contribution of one or more functions.

Perhaps the most important reason for valuing all the functions is accepting advice from function leaders on business issues.

For example, Tiegen is a newly appointed business leader who came up through production. James, the sales leader, is requesting approval for special pricing to entice a major new customer to sign up. That customer is considering other offers and wants a quick resolution. James explains the situation and likely benefits. Tiegen doesn't know enough about selling or the likely customer and can't evaluate the risks properly. Relying on James's judgment right now is the most likely way to land this customer. Tiegen doesn't like James because of disagreements they've had in the past. He also thinks the sales force is only concerned with their commissions, not the business. So, he says no. The sale is lost. Tiegen wouldn't accept the reality that James had superior knowledge.

A business leader once said to us, "I've spent my whole life avoiding legal and HR. Now they report to me. What do I do?" Typically, this sentiment comes from having had a bad experience or a bad relationship with the function. This leader's feelings came from HR having blocked an important promotion and from working with a particularly rigid legal function leader. It's astonishing that a leader can arrive at business manager level without learning the value of support functions such as finance, HR, legal, audit, and credit.

Without this understanding, business leaders often ignore or reject these functions, much to the detriment of them and the business. Good support organizations provide useful analyses and reports, serve as early warning on problems, and provide advice from their perspective. They are the ones who are first to identify cost and revenue problems, unrest in the workforce and leadership ranks, and risks being taken knowingly or unknowingly. Because they support the whole organization, they can be the eyes and ears of the business leader for activities and problems below the business team.

Time Application

It is obvious from the job to be done that rational, not emotional, time management is needed for success as a business leader. Letting go of highly valued function work, such as developing function strategy, problem-solving, and pursuing state-of-the-art technology, is a must. The volume of items to be accounted for, directly or through direct reports, requires careful use of time to manage the complexity.

Thinking time for considering strategy development and related investment decisions is a top priority. To make sure this happens, day-to-day activity must be put aside for at least some part of each day. Some of this think time is done alone and some with the business team. How much time is spent thinking is definable but clearly many business leaders aren't spending enough.

It would not be unusual for a business leader to spend 50% of their time on people issues. Current problems such as retention problems, quiet quitting, and feelings of being excluded require attention from all leaders. Because the business leader is the most visible and powerful leader, the time spent on people issues can be particularly effective. Succession planning, performance evaluation, coaching, and so on all deserve serious amounts of time. The number of people in the business affects the time required where smaller employee counts require less time.

Skills

Few people are prepared for the avalanche of accountability that comes with the business leader role. Not only are many duties unfamiliar but also the sheer volume of unfamiliar things is daunting. The skill required to properly make the connections is often called "a nose for profit." Both short-term and long-term profit-making skills are required. Learning how all the pieces fit together is critical. *Finding opportunities* for business growth and operational improvement is a big part of connecting the dots.

If this were only linear learning, it would be more manageable. Now the learning is three dimensional. Conceptually, the challenge is to *make the right connections* among diverse people, resources, assets, activities, and processes. This connecting the dots requirement isn't child's play. It requires business leaders to see both short-term and long-term connections. For example, entry-level recruiting must not only fill jobs now but also eventually produce employees who can be function and business leaders. Hiring should be followed quickly by development. Development takes time and money in most cases, so what should the business manager give up and when in order to build the right development capability?

Finding the right combination of product offering, price, quality, service, and delivery requires much *strategic thinking and planning.* Getting the right mix of cost control, customer acquisition, process improvement, technology application, facilities use, and people skills is equally important. The resulting value proposition defines the business's purpose. This purpose becomes a guiding force for all leaders and employees. Suppliers and customers benefit from knowing the purpose, so it must be *communicated to a broad audience.* Competitors add to the complexity by never standing still. They too want a competitive advantage so their actions change the playing field, which often requires adjustment to the value proposition.

The real secret to managing this complexity is *building a team of functional leaders* willing to share the burden. To be successful they must work together and focus on the business, not just their own function. Valuing an integrated business team and spending the time needed to build one is one of the most important new business leader priorities. It doesn't usually happen on its own. It won't happen at all if the business manager doesn't value all the functions equally. High-quality function managers won't take the job or stay in the job if they are made to feel like second-class citizens.

One Hundred Plus Elements Found in Most Businesses

Advertising	Furniture	Processes
Affiliates	Goals	Products
Analytics	Goodwill	Profit
Assets	Ideas	Projects
Authority	Individual	Programs
Automobiles	contributors	Prospective
Bad debts	Innovation	customers
Benefits	Insurance	Purpose
Bills	Intellectual capital	Raw materials
Blueprints	Intranet	Real estate
Bonds	Inventory	Receivables
Brand	Jobs	Reports
Cash	Job descriptions	Reputation
Checks	Knowledge	Research
Commitments	Laboratories	Revenue
Communication	Liabilities	Rewards
Community	Licenses	Risk
Community	Leaders	Rules
involvement	Ledgers	Secrets
Competitors	Licensees	Services
Computers	Logistics	Stock
Consumers	Logos	Strategy
Contractors	Market position	Suppliers
Costs	Measurements	Supplies
Credit	Memberships	Systems
Culture	Mission	Technology
Copyrights	Mortgages	Threats
Customers	Networks	Titles
Data	Offices	Trademarks
Energy	Organization	Training
Ethics	Owners	Unions
Experience	Partners	Vision
Expertise	Patents	Warehouses
Factories	Pensions	Warranties
Furnishings	Plans	

Source: Copyright Drotter Human Resources, Inc.

Typical Transition Issues

Identifying those who are having trouble with this leadership passage requires informed observation. The signs and symptoms aren't always obvious. If they are having trouble with complexity, they won't go around saying so. In fact, they are more likely to cover it up. Figure 6.4 shows some of the most common signs of struggle with this passage, and these are discussed in the next sections.

Failing to Let Go of the Function Leader Mindset

When you see a frenetic business leader who rockets from project to project and never has enough time to spend with any of the key people, you are observing a clear sign of trouble at this leadership layer. New business leaders often have difficulty finding a balance among working on strategy, visiting customers, connecting externally, building their team, and so on. They are still working as though they are function managers. Instead of just lending their ear to the function managers and being their sparring partner, they try to solve all problems in all functions themselves. They act as

Typical Transition Issues

- Failing to let go of the function leader mindset
- Inability to assemble a strong management team
- Failing to grasp how the business makes money
- Neglecting the soft issues
- Failing to grasp how digitization and AI will affect the business

Figure 6.4. Typical Transition Issues for Business Leaders.
Source: Copyright Leadership Pipeline Institute.

function leader for all the functions instead of being the business leader orchestrating the organization. We call this working *in the business* not *on the business*. Building a strong team and letting them handle the tactical work is the missing requirement. Prioritizing from the whole business point of view and delivering results on an appropriate short-term and long-term basis require working on the business.

A related sign of poor transition in this area is the business leader stepping in to run critical projects or programs just as they did as a function leader. When they take "personal responsibility," they are trying to run the business through products or technology rather than through their people and organization. The responsible function leader is marginalized. This might make the new business leader look and feel heroic, but it takes time away from the critical strategy and integration work.

In many organizations, leadership pipelines are clogged with business leaders who retreat from the complexity of their new positions. Rather than take the time and expend the mental energy necessary to grasp the situations confronting them, they fall back on familiar leadership approaches.

Case study

Gary is an example of someone who embraced rather than retreated from complexity when he was named a business leader by his giant financial services organization. For 10 years Gary had moved through a series of increasingly difficult assignments in the company's commodity trading business. He had done well, and when his boss was promoted, Gary replaced him as business leader. It was an expected promotion because Gary's business was considered one of the best in the world and he had a great deal to do with its success.

Gary's boss had also been very successful in running that business. So when Gary took over he could have easily maintained the strategy of his predecessor. Revenue was about $500 million and the business enjoyed an excellent 23.8% operating margin. Gary, however, was not about to assume anything about the business. He used three baskets as a tool to evaluate, understand, and connect strategic direction, collective individual competence, and organizational competence. He also was willing to ask his direct reports and customers questions that betrayed his "ignorance."

What he discovered was that the industry was in an overcapacity position, the value of traditional products was declining, and the anticipated market turn down was about to become a reality and reduce the demand for his products. His global business was strong in Europe but weakening in North America and Asia. Talent in the business wasn't distributed evenly and goals were poorly integrated. Working closely with his team, Gary came to the conclusion that the current business model was not in line with current realities and customer needs.

Inability to Assemble a Strong Management Team

Building the right team is crucial at this level because of the complexity, unfamiliarity with some functions, and the volume of work. Nonetheless some business leaders persist in being a one-person gang. A common symptom of this mentality is failure to build an effective team of direct reports. Typically, the business leader favors one function (usually the one in which they grew up) and alienates the others. It is also possible they don't know enough about some functions to recruit and hire a competent leader. Sometimes they don't provide enough encouragement and clear expectations necessary for function leaders to work together. When weak function leaders are inherited and not replaced, the other team members resist interacting with them. When these conditions exist, there can be an undercurrent of mistrust when the function managers meet so teamwork required for business success isn't likely. When function leader teams are contentious, disrespectful, and ineffectual, it is a sign that the new business leader's transition isn't working.

Failing to Grasp How the Business Makes Money

This is a transition challenge we experience mainly when business leaders are promoted to run a business in which they did not grow up. The business leaders' accountability is for delivering profit, both short term and long term, with high capital efficiency. Many new business leaders just don't get what the profit improvement requirements are. Though they may understand the requirements on one level, they aren't able to translate them into appropriate action. For example, a new business leader from operations or finance may not be confident in customer situations because they aren't familiar enough with sales and marketing activities. So they become obsessed with customer calls, falsely assuming this is the key to profit. Rather than seeing the entire profit chain, they focus only on one piece and end up undermining the sales function.

Just as significantly, this failure to recognize where profit comes from may be the result of not knowing the core business processes. Understanding takes work. It means asking lots of questions and admitting ignorance. Developing trusted advisors who can fill in the blanks is a key part. Transitioning from a function they know like the back of their hand to a multifunctional job with a sea of unknowns is very challenging. It is tempting for some to bluff their way through rather than invest the time and energy required, and sacrifice their ego, in order to know what core processes are needed to win. Effective business leaders possess sufficient self-confidence to admit where they lack knowledge and demonstrate a willingness to shift assignments to people who have the knowledge.

Neglecting the Soft Issues

Business leaders who ignore cultural issues haven't learned to value the power an appropriate culture can have in helping the business run smoothly. As a result, they avoid spending time and energy shaping the culture the business needs. Being the custodian of the culture is a new responsibility for these leaders, and their reaction may be to ignore it or give it a low priority even if the existing culture is no longer appropriate. Tackling a culture change is time-consuming and difficult so it can get pushed aside.

Failing to Grasp How Digitization and AI Will Affect the Business

Digitization can be a business leader's best friend or worst enemy. If they stay abreast of developments and have the courage to invest in technology and the flexibility to alter strategy to get full use of the investment, competitive advantage is possible. Equally possible is falling behind competition through a lack of awareness and failure to invest. Ridged adherence to existing, tried-and-true use out of ignorance or a lack of courage to invest creates a blind spot for technology. Competitive disadvantage will soon follow.

It is broadly accepted by business leaders that digitization and AI are important to keep track of. Where we see the difference is how business leaders act on the opportunities/threats. Almost all business leaders we meet have initiated what we could call incremental digitization, meaning that they look for cost/operational improvements and they digitize some internal data and some processes. The blind spot appears when they believe that with these incremental initiatives they are now in the game. Often, they are not in the game. They are not even close to entering the game.

Although they drive their "incremental improvement" agenda, competitors are reassessing their entire business model. They are identifying opportunities for extracting all types of data from their products to the benefit of their business and their clients. Competitors are creating new products based on data and they are entering markets that were previously not accessible to them.

These major digitization agendas have to be sponsored by the CEO as they will ultimately transform the entire business they are leading.

In Chapter 7 we will discuss the enterprise leader role. Many business leaders are also the enterprise leader, which adds another significant layer to the job.

7

Leading an Enterprise

Agreat deal of recognition surrounds this leadership passage, as
well as a great deal of failure. When new enterprise leaders
are named, usually called chief executive officer (CEO), newspaper
articles are written about them, their appointment is hailed by
friends and colleagues, and their social calendars fill up quickly.
Many enterprise leaders develop a large presence in national and
world media. Within a few years of their appointment, however,
many chief executives are gone or on their way out. Over the last
five years the turnover has accelerated almost beyond belief. These
aren't stupid people. In fact, many failed enterprise leaders are
brilliant strategists and visionaries. Nonetheless, they lacked the
work values, time application, and skills demanded at this leadership level. They may not have had an enterprise mindset.

Note: Previous editions of this book included discussion of
leading a group. But this role seems to be disappearing. As
organizations flatten and information flows to the bottom
through digitization, much of the work formally associated
with the group leader is now handled by the enterprise leader.
We discuss the group leader in more detail in Chapter 11.

Technological advances have spawned hundreds of new businesses in areas such as software and applications, medical breakthroughs, medicine and drugs, cash management, leadership coaching, new services, and so on. Many of them are small start-ups with a handful of employees. They all have an enterprise leader. The concepts in this book apply to them in a different way. We will discuss this later in the chapter.

Successful enterprise leaders exhibit sound judgment on people matters and execute well deep into the organization. Though strategic ability, vision, and other factors are important skills at this level of leadership, they won't rescue an enterprise leader who can't get things done or who lacks the ability to put the right person in the right job or who can't build relationships. What makes the transition to enterprise manager so difficult is that they're managing an enterprise in its totality, not just a business, and are responsible to multiple constituencies—boards, investors, alliance partners, the workforce, shareholders, direct reports, local communities, and so on. More than any other leader, they're under internal and external microscopes.

In very big companies the enterprise leaders have business leaders reporting to them as well as corporate function leaders. Choosing, developing, and leading effective business leaders is an important part of their job. In order to make the right choice, spending sufficient time with the function leaders—those reporting to the business leaders—to learn their strengths, capabilities, weaknesses, and career ambitions is a must. Collaborating with the existing business leaders and the corporate function leaders on planning development for function leaders to test their promotability is a core responsibility. That responsibility receives too little effort in many, many cases. If the enterprise leader chooses a business manager who fails, the enterprise leader suffers the consequences. It is in the enterprise leader's best interest to establish an effective succession planning system, value the succession planning work, and give it the time it deserves.

In mid-size companies the enterprise leaders are also the business leader, and the function leaders report to them. Molding the function leaders into a high-performing team is an important responsibility because ultimately the success of the business depends on it. Having function leaders pull together to achieve business results is the objective. Because functions have different interests, different technologies, different states-of-the-art, and different talent needs, it is easy for them to pull in different directions. A compelling vision or strategy is needed.

In small companies, enterprise leaders often have leading-self (technical and professional) people reporting to them. Enterprise leaders who are also leading others have the same requirements in addition to business and enterprise challenges. Meeting performance requirements, accepting the values, and teamwork are the major needs. It is common for enterprise leaders who are also leading others to get consumed with developing the product and getting it sold. Everything else, such as planning beyond one year, developing their people, making their direct report into a team, doesn't get done.

Case study

Paul was enterprise leader of a business that made wonderful baked goods. He had about 40 full-time employees and two operating locations, one of which doubled as a part-time retail outlet. Two of his direct reports had part-time leadership roles but spent most of their time working on making or selling the product. His numerous customers were primarily retailers who sold his baked goods. They were loyal supporters of the product and were asking for more of them. Paul concluded that he needed to expand production capacity to meet the growing demand for his products. He obtained a sizeable mortgage loan from a local bank and made a down payment on a small abandoned facility in a mixed-use area. His idea was to make it a rustic center for production and retail selling. His customers and friends were excited about the prospect of more product availability.

As required by law, he applied for reconstruction permits from the city and the county. People living near the abandoned site put up a major fuss. They felt there would be too much noise and traffic. They feared their neighborhood would lose its aesthetics and property values would drop. They protested loudly and vigorously at county supervisor meetings and city council meetings. They submitted more than 100 questions to both councils and demanded answers.

Paul hired a lawyer and a publicist to address the neighbors' questions and create a positive publicity campaign. The neighbors came up with another 100 questions. Two years and $500,000 later, reconstruction still hasn't started. The city liked the project but didn't feel they could approve it until the county said okay. The county council appeared to be siding with the individual citizens.

Paul had exhibited business and functional thinking. His focus on the product and the customers was appropriate, but it wasn't enough. He had not considered the community impact. He misjudged the political issues. Enterprise thinking would have included those missing elements.

The Job to Be Done

As one would expect, the enterprise leader's role is the most expansive one in a company. The time line goes out much further and the scale includes almost everything. Because of the length and breadth of the job, great successes are possible. So are great failures. (See Figure 7.1.)

The price of making errors for most enterprise leaders is severe. Missing three or four quarters of earning expectations usually

The Work	Required Activities
Develop an enterprise vision	• Establish enterprise strategic framework. • Define enterprise mission. • Gain acceptance throughout the organization.
Sustain profitability	• Set earnings and investment goals. • Establish a climate of commitment. • Allocate capital across the business units.
Execute excellence	• Build effective organization structure. • Set standards for efficiency. • Conduct regular strategy reviews.
Build social architecture	• Define appropriate enterprise culture. • Communicate and engage everyone. • Create room for diversity.
Lead globally	• Monitor world events. • Engage relevant global leaders. • Support ESG initiatives.

Figure 7.1. Leading an Enterprise: The Job to Be Done.
Source: Copyright Leadership Pipeline Institute.

results in significant negative publicity, which travels across the internet instantly. For smaller companies, their investors have very little patience.

As mentioned, we've seen people become enterprise leaders quickly, without obtaining the appropriate experience. They've skipped some of the passages that prepare people to be successful enterprise leaders. They often display a lack of appreciation for the complexity of required solutions. When faced with new issues or uncertain conditions they lack the experience to construct meaningful solutions. For some people, especially those who have not experienced much failure in their work lives, this can be a shock.

Lack of experience isn't necessarily linked to age. Successful young enterprise leaders are emerging in information technology, biotech start-ups of all kinds, personal services, and health care, to name a few. In knowledge worker industries, people are moving to the top at unprecedented speed. As a result, they must transition from one leadership level to the next very quickly. Bright, young 24-year-olds can create companies, attract the best people, and hype their stock.

For some, the lack of experience through the leadership passages eventually catches up with them. When they don't have the right people or the right team, they don't meet the demands of investors and shareholders. Getting there fast without training and sufficient experience is highly risky for the enterprise as well as the individual. In addition, today's business leaders in big companies don't have the group executive–level experience, which was common in the early 2000s, as a developmental passage. Moving to flatter organization structures has taken away the group leader layer in many companies, reducing the opportunity for development.

Developing an Enterprise Mindset

If a new enterprise leader has progressed through the pipeline passages, important business considerations have already been in focus. Profit, competitive advantage, employees, customers, products, investors, suppliers, communities, and so on have all been important in their thinking. Some have had higher priority than others, some have been secondary. Now these elements are all of significance. As enterprise leader the required mindset is "everything counts." The danger is continuing to think customers are more important than employees or profit is more important than products. This is harder than it sounds, particularly after having success at one or two of these.

To elaborate on each category of work in turn: enterprise leaders do whatever is needed to perpetuate the enterprise without compromising their values.

Enterprise Leaders Create an Enterprise Vision

Vision, strategic acumen, and positioning know-how are all crucial skills for setting a company on course for long-term success.

On top of this, digitization has added a layer of complication and uncertainty. Information and access have changed even the most basic business processes. The product or service itself, how it is made, how it is purchased, and how it is delivered are all subjected to rapid change driven by new technology and access to information. And so leaders must find a way to set their enterprise vision in this digital age.

The enterprise leader must decide where to take the company, what recipes or business models will make money, and what competitive patterns to heed. It's also important to identify the current assumptions about changes in the industry or field and to verify if those views need to be updated. The enterprise leaders in every major industry, for example, automotive, software, news, health care, social media, entertainment companies, and many others, are wrestling with this positioning challenge right now and will continue to do so.

Meeting this challenge requires more than a vision statement. Many companies have such statements and hang them on their walls. Most of these visions are so broad and unfocused that they are meaningless. As an experiment, collect the statements for 50 companies; you'll find that they're remarkably similar. The real challenge for the enterprise leader is to craft a concrete definition of where to take the enterprise. At the very least, this demands that an enterprise leader display real courage in making tough choices. Such courage has been displayed by the enterprise leaders who repositioned 20th-century stalwarts such as IBM, GE, DeBeers, and DuPont for success in the 21st century. These are now very different businesses than they used to be. In a very real sense, this leadership passage requires enterprise leaders to value tasks that they've never done before, and that can be scary. More than one enterprise leader has told us that this is the first time they felt a lack of confidence in their ability to set strategic direction. Valuing the risk-taking, taking the time required for deep thinking, and unraveling complexities at this level all are crucial if enterprise leaders are to be successful.

Enterprise Leaders Enable Sustained Profitability

In any publicly held company, enterprise leaders are evaluated by investors and security analysts on a quarterly basis. The scorecards are posted hourly on stock exchanges. Every quarter, Wall Street publishes expectations of both top-line and bottom-line growth. Any slip in meeting those expectations and delivery of results detracts from the enterprise leader's credibility, their most important asset. To survive, enterprise leaders must learn to value short-term and long-term results, develop the skill to balance both, and invest the time required to achieve this balance. Delivering consistent, predictable top-line and bottom-line results is the hallmark of great enterprise leaders.

Growing into this role doesn't happen overnight. In most instances, people who make the transition successfully have gone through all the earlier leadership pipeline passages. They've learned how to make increasingly bigger trade-offs at each level. They've developed the ability to anticipate long-term ramifications and adjust short-term tactics with the long term in mind. Over time, they've become adept at seeing the larger picture, dealing with multiple constituencies, and communicating. At some point, they've acquired the emotional fortitude necessary to make unpleasant decisions.

Enterprise Leaders Maintain Execution Excellence

Contrary to popular belief, enterprise leaders don't need to be strategic wizards or brilliant visionaries to succeed. They do, however, need to get things done. Enterprise leaders who are indecisive or don't deliver on commitments are the ones whose organizations suffer; they're also the ones who are asked by their boards to leave.

Execution is more critical for enterprise leaders now than in years past. Just about every industry is more competitive because of technology and global markets. Talent shortages of all kinds have affected execution. Information technology has empowered customers in ways that make it even more important for organizations to sell the steak rather than the sizzle. As a result, enterprise leaders can't simply talk a good game. At other leadership levels, they may have been able to get by with flawed execution. At this level, the flaws will destroy an enterprise leader.

Valuing execution isn't always easy for enterprise leaders. The nitty-gritty details of getting things done aren't the most glamorous aspects of the job. The best enterprise leaders, however, recognize that this is where the payoff is for themselves as enterprise leaders and for their organizations. Those who maintain an execution edge continually ask themselves the following questions:

How's my performance? To answer this question positively, enterprise leaders develop performance forecasts for the next eight quarters (not just the usual four). Early on, they start thinking about performance-focused changes they may need to make down the line.

Do I know what's going on? Execution requires the latest information from the most important sources. Enterprise leaders should be directly connected to customers and front-line employees and be well informed about how the company and the markets are doing. It was done physically it the past but much of it can be done electronically now. Customer surveys are commonplace in many industries so data and opinions are available. The follow-up is what matters, and enterprise leaders have an obligation to do so as part of a business effectiveness responsibility.

Are people telling me the bad news? In some organizations, people are afraid to give the enterprise leader bad news. At others, enterprise leaders are unwilling to hear the bad news, rationalizing every negative report. Enterprise leaders can't execute properly if they let bad news build to the crisis point. By the time they're willing to listen it may be too late.

Is the board fulfilling its mandate? If they're just a rubber stamp, they're hampering the enterprise leader's ability to achieve results. When they hold the enterprise leader and their direct reports accountable and ask for information about productivity, succession, customer satisfaction, and the company's markets, for example, they're focusing the enterprise leader's attention on execution.

Is my team productive and enthusiastic? When an enterprise leader's team is divisive and inconsistent, it is often a sign that the enterprise leader is in trouble. When the team can't achieve consensus and accomplish a relatively simple goal, it's likely that the enterprise leader is having trouble producing acceptable results.

Do we have the right technology in place? Organizations can go to extremes when considering use of technology. Some try every new thing that comes along, usually at great expense. Some rigidly hold to existing technology and related processes to avoid risks. Either way the organization won't function properly and the enterprise leader is in trouble.

To complete this leadership passage successfully, enterprise leaders must shift their work values, time application, and skills in the direction of execution. This means they must develop an insatiable appetite for accomplishment and results. It means they must understand the business deeply, acquiring an almost instinctive sense of how the company makes money. It means they must spend a great deal of time diagnosing whether the organization is performing at full potential. And it means they must become skilled at converting learning into practice, identifying the best ideas, and translating them into tools and programs that benefit the organization.

Enterprise Leaders Build Social Architecture

Every company is a social organization. When two or more people work together, they inevitably develop a relationship of some kind.

Maintaining a culture in which such relationships evolve constructively is a crucial responsibility of the enterprise leader. They are responsible for shaping the soft side of the enterprise. If teamwork and mutual support are valued, those relationships can flourish. Focusing on these soft issues while also striving for hard business results is a juggling act not every enterprise leader can handle.

More so than ever before, enterprise leaders must energize people: releasing this energy at all levels and particularly at the lowest level, where the action is. Communicating in ways that energize large and diverse groups of employees is a soft skill that enterprise leaders must learn to value and master. Transparency, candor, and openness to feedback are foundational.

No company can prosper without having the right people in the right jobs, especially at a time when leading-edge skills can become obsolete in the wink of an eye (or a change in technology). Selecting the right people and continuously upgrading their skills and knowledge ultimately is a responsibility that falls on the enterprise leader. Although others may carry out the technical aspects of selection and development, the enterprise leader must initiate, maintain, and manage the process, for leaders in particular, by continuously asking questions such as these:

- Do I have the right executive team?

- What can I do to improve development of leaders across the enterprise?

- Where can we move decision-making authority to lower levels to attract the best people?

- How good are we at selecting the right people?

- How candid is our feedback and how frequently is it given? What should our standards be?

- How willing are we to end mismatches between jobs and people in a timely fashion?

- How vigilant are we in retaining high performers, moving them faster, rewarding them appropriately, and giving them realistic opportunities to test themselves?

- Are we giving enough consideration to work/ life balance?

Succession planning, selection, rewards, recruitment, performance management, retention, communication, and safety are examples of the systems needed. The enterprise leader makes sure they are in place and work properly.

Enterprise Leaders Lead Globally

No company can survive without paying attention to the community and the world around it. Just as every organization takes from the community, it must also give back. Organizations should be aware and active in solving the social problems that confront them. They must pay attention to and take position on preserving the environment, ensuring public and employee safety and health issues, equitable hiring practices, and inclusive organizations. Every enterprise leader must know their constituency, be they environmentalists or social justice advocates or other special interest groups. Many enterprise leaders come to their jobs lacking knowledge or experience in these areas. They may never have thought enough about how their organization is affecting global warming or whether they are likely to face the consequences of a war. In fact, many enterprise leaders have told us that they don't have a handle on how to deal with various special interest groups whose modus operandi and base of power are very different from their own. In attempting to lead the company in a broader, global context, they find the experience to be foreign in figurative and literal senses. Yet to make an effective transition to this leadership level, enterprise leaders must adapt their thinking and values to this broader context.

The Transition to the Role

We have displayed the required transition of work values, time application, and skills from the previous layer compared to the new layer in specific terms. There are many previous layers for those becoming enterprise leaders. Some move from business leader to enterprise leader. At the other extreme some move from leading self as an engineer or salesperson to enterprise leader. For many of these transitions only a few of the enterprise requirements apply so we display only the enterprise leader requirements in Figure 7.2.

In smaller companies that have only two, three, or four layers there are some critical enterprise-level requirements. Valuing enterprise excellence is important for every enterprise leader, no matter how small the enterprise might be.

For anyone who is a leader-of-others or leader-of-leaders and business leader and enterprise leader, the transition challenge

Leading an Enterprise

WORK VALUES
- Enterprise results
- Enterprise excellence in all areas
- Valuing different business models
- Continuous learning

TIME APPLICATION
- Culture building
- External presence and relationship building
- Communication to broad audiences

SKILLS
- Visionary thinking
- Executive-level team building
- Relationship building with key external leaders and the board

Figure 7.2. Work Values, Time Application, and Skills for Enterprise Leaders.

Source: Copyright Leadership Pipeline Institute.

centers on the time line. It is easy to get caught up in the day-to-day challenges. To make sure there will be a future, time must be applied to longer term thinking and planning. Spending time monitoring relevant external trends is necessary for doing longer term planning. Assessing the future implications of current events is the starting point.

For function leaders who are also enterprise leaders, changing time lines is important to them as well. Visionary thinking, which is quite different from creating function strategy, is the key requirement. Moving to enterprise excellence from functional excellence requires consideration of a much broader range of elements.

For business leaders who are also enterprise leaders, it is essential they take the time to build external relationships and board relationships. Visionary thinking, which is quite different from strategic thinking, must be learned.

Work Values

Given the major challenges enterprise leaders face as they make this leadership transition, they must adapt their values accordingly—and this role calls for a significant shift in work values. As we've suggested, enterprise leadership demands a system of beliefs substantially different from what is required at other leadership levels. Though we've discussed some of the work values that prove necessary to enterprise leaders, we'd like to focus here on the larger value shift that must take place.

Up until this point, most leaders have learned to value short-term and medium-term operating results (one to three years) and regular, measurable achievements. Though they may recognize the need for long-term planning and goals if they've successfully navigated previous leadership levels, they often find it difficult to accept the pace at which enterprise results happen. Achieving a culture change or implementing a new quality program can take a long time to be fully realized. For leaders who have built their careers achieving results faster and more effectively than their peers, valuing big but slow and evolutionary results can be a struggle. And so, for example, a common enterprise leader failing is giving up on long-cycle programs (such as installing new technology or expanding into new territory) before they're fully implemented and producing measurable results.

Similarly, many enterprise leaders experience difficulty valuing only three or four key objectives. Business leaders frequently have long lists of goals. They derive satisfaction by checking off one item after the next. The enterprise leader, however, should derive satisfaction from a short list of long-cycle initiatives. Changing brand identity, for example, can take years. In a very real sense, the shift in values is from immediate gratification to sustained progress. Enterprise leaders recognize that the most ambitious and significant objectives take time to achieve, and they learn to live without the quick fix of immediate achievement that characterizes other leadership levels in favor of more slowly but surely working toward a major success. The confounding paradox, of course, is that side by side with this patience is the need to deliver quarter-by-quarter commitments. They resolve this paradox by learning to get certain things done fast and others slowly, and they make sure they don't confuse the two (for instance, getting things done slowly that need to be done fast). Finding the balance between the short term and the long term and executing it is what makes enterprise leaders successful.

Another problematic value shift involves taking advice from boards. For people who are accustomed to running their own business in a multi-business company, this value can be an obstacle. In the past, leaders may have received advice from peers, coaches, or bosses, but boards are a different breed of advice giver. Board members' opinions may seem superficial or less informed than an insider's perspective. Also, directors as individuals may provide conflicting advice, and some enterprise leaders will devalue that advice simply because they're perplexed by it. We've found, however, that enterprise leaders who are open with their boards, and make an effort to listen and learn from them, ultimately benefit in their decision-making. If the board is unable to provide informed advice, the enterprise leader's responsibility is to educate them until they're able to do so.

Finally, the best enterprise leaders learn to value asking questions and listening to a broad spectrum of people. This is almost a counterintuitive value, given the power that comes with the enterprise leader's position and the ego that's required to obtain it. In fact, a significant percentage of enterprise leaders have risen from one leadership level to the next based on their strong, aggressive style and their ability to wield power. Power, however, becomes dysfunctional when enterprise leaders don't exercise restraint. Although enterprise leaders possess ultimate position power, true leaders at this level don't rely exclusively on position power to get things done. They recognize that influence can get things done with energy and innovation rather than just with grudging compliance. Influential enterprise leaders share their vision with a variety of people in order to capture their interest and motivate them to help.

The dictatorial, ego-driven enterprise leader tends not to ask many questions or listen to the answers. They value their own opinion above all others, and as a result they tune out ideas and perspectives that clash with their own. Although most new enterprise leaders don't fit the dictatorial prototype, many do not fully value listening to multiple perspectives. Too often, a new enterprise leader relies on one trusted advisor rather than the team and the board.

Time Application

Because their accountability is for the entire enterprise, enterprise leaders' time must be spent on activities that affect the entire enterprise. Company culture is becoming more and more important as a tool for binding the organization together. How employees behave toward each other and the world around them marks the enterprise as a good citizen or a poor one. Changing behavior for individuals from a self-focus to a citizenship focus is accomplished by establishing a well-defined culture. Understanding what the culture is now, defining what it should be, and undertaking the necessary programs to instill any needed changes is a critical use of time for enterprise leaders.

Connecting the enterprise to the world around it by building necessary relationships, engaging with appropriate external organizations, and communicating the enterprise message to broad audiences are actions only the enterprise leader can perform. Enabling the team to help build this external presence is necessary to get all the work done.

Communication with employees, customers, shareholders, the board, the public, and various governments to make clear what the enterprise is trying to accomplish and to learn what these audiences expect requires deliberate planning and crafting of messages.

Skills

Creating a vision of what the enterprise can be or should be is something only the enterprise leader can do. Most new enterprise leaders find this is bigger thinking than they are used to, and it is seldomly done correctly on the first try. Testing the thinking with key people and evolving the picture is the way the skill is developed. This visionary thinking is an iterative process, and is fundamental to both defining the company culture and shaping the external presence.

Building the direct reports into an executive team can be a difficult challenge. The direct reports have personal ambition, competing interests, and the need for compromise—all of which will challenge the enterprise leader and require some skill development. The enterprise leader has no choice but to develop this skill because so many other requirements of the job require teamwork. Of course, it's likely that the enterprise leader has built teams in the past. But in this role the task can be harder because the team members are experienced and successful people who may not agree that teamwork is in their best interest.

Relationship skill building isn't new for most enterprise leaders. The new challenge is heavily focused on external people who have major leadership positions. These external leaders have their own agendas and may not be enthusiastic about accepting what the enterprise leader is trying to do. Perhaps the most important relationship is with the board—gaining the board's confidence is the highest priority. The enterprise leader and the board want the same thing, but they may not agree on how to get it. If they spend enough time together, they can often work out any differences.

Typical Transition Issues

The most obvious sign is a downward financial spiral that occurs under the new enterprise leader's watch. Although a financial crisis may not be caused specifically by an enterprise leader experiencing difficulties with this leadership transition, their response (or lack thereof) to the crisis may signal transition problems. In many instances, however, the signs are a bit more subtle. (See Figure 7.3.)

Failing to Connect with How the Enterprise Operates

This goes back to the challenge of maintaining an edge in execution. Sometimes new enterprise leaders just don't get it—*it* being how the place works. In conversations and by their actions, they demonstrate their ignorance of what is required to get the right people in the right jobs or to implement a new program or policy. They don't understand how to use their influence to pull the right levers to overcome inertia or fight through other obstacles to get results. Either they're not interested in learning how the enterprise executes or they're content with their false assumptions. In either case, they make little or no effort to examine and review operations in all businesses, to listen to people at every level, and to obtain

Typical Transition Issues

- Failing to connect with how the enterprise operates
- Focusing on external relationships
- Avoiding the soft side of the enterprise
- Failing to sufficiently answer board members' questions
- Refusing to consider other business models
- Leading the business instead of leading the business leaders

Figure 7.3. Typical Transition Issues for Leaders-of-Enterprises.
Source: Copyright Leadership Pipeline Institute.

the customer's view of service and quality. Signs of disinterest in these issues are relatively subtle. Overt signs are financial, and deterioration in earnings signals that an enterprise leader is walking toward the brink. We know of at least four enterprise leaders who didn't have the faintest idea about how their enterprise executes, and the result was at least a $1 billion loss in each instance. When a new enterprise leader is blindsided with significant operating shortfalls, it's often a sign that they don't understand how things get done.

Although the enterprise leader of a company with fewer than 200 employees may understand enterprise execution if they've been there a few years, in a bigger company, or a rapidly growing organization, or one in a complex industry, the learning curve is steeper. Enterprise leaders who isolate themselves from a range of people and information or leave execution to others are not making this leadership turn.

Focusing on External Activities

It's not that customer functions, government meetings, community events, celebrity golf tournaments, and the like are unimportant. Part of the enterprise leader's role is interacting with external groups and projecting a positive public image for themselves and the enterprise. This is seductive activity, however, and some enterprise leaders lose sight of the larger leadership responsibilities at this level. Specifically, they fail to see that no one's minding the store. Enterprise leaders should spend their time in a balanced way on external and internal issues. If the balance tips in one direction—especially when it's in an external direction—then something is wrong. Enterprise leaders who get caught up in acting the part rather than being the chief executive often find themselves and their company in hot water.

Avoiding the Soft Side of the Enterprise

The people issues can be terribly complex from an enterprise leader's perspective, and some enterprise leaders find it easier to deal with product issues instead. For instance, they are in charge of the leadership pipeline, and if they show no interest in selecting and developing leadership at all levels in all parts of the enterprise, it is a sure sign that the soft side of the business is not sufficiently important. Some enterprise leaders maintain the traditional enterprise culture even though it is no longer useful. Similarly, some people reach enterprise leader positions and immediately appoint their buddies to key jobs, surrounding themselves with friends. Though enterprise leader certainly is entitled to select a team of people they know and trust, any form of corporate nepotism sends the wrong message throughout the organization. It demotivates strong performers and encourages noncritical responses to superiors instead of honest dialogue. Enterprise leaders should establish a process and requirements for filling key positions. They should also make sure the company's culture is appropriate for the business and the times. Changing the culture is difficult and time consuming so many enterprise leaders avoid doing it. If they don't, they're demonstrating an aversion to soft matters.

Failing to Sufficiently Answer Board Members' Questions

When results are below expectations and shareholders are scrutinizing a company closely, board members feel the pressure and begin to ask hard questions of the enterprise leader. If the enterprise leader isn't answering the questions satisfactorily and the same questions are asked at several board meetings, it's a sign of trouble. Even if boards are generally not the rubber stamps of the past, they're rarely adversarial. A disharmonious relationship with the board often means that the enterprise leader lacks a key skill or doesn't possess appropriate values for this leadership position.

Refusing to Consider Other Business Models

Enterprise leaders in large companies often have multiple business or different business lines within the company. Most enterprise leaders grow up in one or a maximum of two different business lines in their way to the position. They get to know the business model and how to make money in that one business unit. As enterprise leaders, they are now in charge of all the business units within the company. Different types of business often require very different business models, different reward systems, different ways of competing. A simple example is very large banks. They often consist of three, four, or five of the following business lines: consumer banking (retail), corporate banking, investment banking, real estate financing, mortgage lending, leasing, and correspondent banking. These are all very different businesses. What we have seen in multiple business companies is the enterprise leader trying to enforce one common operating model across the entire company, not leaving room for business-driven differences in the business units. We have also seen that when one business unit is struggling to deliver results, the enterprise leader tries to impose the business model that they themselves are most comfortable with rather than a more appropriate one. The enterprise leader fails to recognize that when business is completely different the requirements are different.

Leading the Business Instead of Leading the Business Leaders

Enterprise leaders provide leadership for their business leaders, including approving their strategies, but they do not run their businesses. This isn't just semantics. Enterprise leaders can be strongly tempted to change a business strategy, challenge pricing, consolidate factories, and do all the "important" things they used to do as business leaders. Although it's critical for them to ask questions and evaluate whether business leaders are carrying out these tasks effectively, they do tremendous damage to the leadership pipeline if they carry out these things themselves. If the business leader is not delivering the results, then the enterprise leader can develop and coach the business leader or select a new business leader. But they should never start running the business themselves. Other important work that only the CEO can do won't get done properly.

Leading an enterprise requires intelligence, but it isn't a paper-and-pencil exercise. Making dazzling electronic presentations to boards isn't what the job is all about. It's really about positioning the company for long-term success, ensuring successful execution, choosing the right people, valuing enterprise results, developing an appropriate culture, and building relationships inside and out. Enterprise leaders who aren't adept at these tasks—who don't have a clue about how to select and nurture leaders or build relationships in all directions—will probably fail no matter how skilled they are at mapping strategy.

If there were only one or two passages in the company, there will be gaps in the CEO's development. Strategy development and long-term thinking, dealing with external forces and building external relationships, and choosing and developing leaders will be the likely deficiencies. Reaching out for help is strongly advised. Board members, industry experts, consultants and consulting firms, coursework, and team-based decision-making can all help. In any case, it is critically important for the new enterprise leader to acknowledge the learning they have missed and be open-minded in hearing suggestions. Outsiders shouldn't make the decisions, just provide advice and information. Decisions should be made by the enterprise leader and the team.

PART III
APPLICATION

8

Strategies for Implementing the Leadership Pipeline Model

Implementing the Leadership Pipeline framework is usually not that challenging. The reason for this is that you already have a leadership pipeline! You have leaders-of-others, leaders-of-leaders, and so forth. In principle, you do not "implement" the Leadership Pipeline model per se in the organization. You apply the Leadership Pipeline model to describe already existing leadership roles within your organization. This description is what we call a Leadership Portrait.

From an implementation perspective you then also need to consider the following:

- Whether you should start with a partial implementation, or if you should immediately go for a full organizational implementation

- How to situate the Leadership Pipeline framework into your existing structures and models

After introducing the Leadership Portrait, we address these questions; at the end of the chapter and provide specific tips for effective implementation.

Designing Leadership Portraits

In Chapters 3 through 7, we outlined the job to be done and the required work values, time application, and skills for the different leadership roles. Combining these two elements gives us what we call the Leadership Portrait. In Figures 8.1 and 8.2 we've illustrated the Leadership Portrait for leaders-of-others.

In Chapter 2, we outlined what business problems you can solve with the Leadership Pipeline model and what results you can achieve. In order to harvest all the benefits from the Leadership Pipeline model, you need a Leadership Portrait in place for each of the defined typical leadership roles/layers within your organization.

The job to be done represents the output of the leadership role. This is what leaders have to deliver, and this is the baseline for holding them accountable and assessing their leadership performance. It should be included in the ongoing performance review of leaders. It also represents the baseline for development. When you develop leaders, and for that matter anyone within the organization, you need to develop them toward something. Otherwise, it becomes empty development plans, and they lose importance from

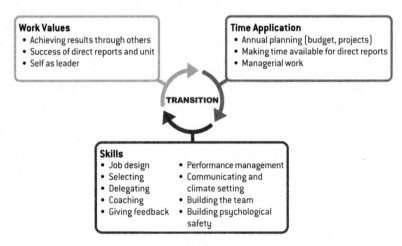

Figure 8.1. Leadership Portrait for Leaders-of-Others (1 of 2).
Source: Copyright Leadership Pipeline Institute.

The Work	Required Activities
Set direction	• Clearly define the roles and priorities of direct reports. • Create a clear understanding of how direct reports' personal business objectives tie into overall team and business-unit objectives. • Engage direct reports in establishing personal business objectives.
Empower	• Enable direct reports to deal effectively with their responsibilities. • Delegate necessary authority to enable direct reports achieving their objectives. • Support direct reports in their work without taking direct ownership of their specific work.
Develop direct reports	• Set specific development objectives for direct reports. • Provide constructive and fact-based feedback. • Continuously include coaching as part of their leadership style.
Follow through on performance of direct reports	• Regularly initiate check-in conversations to support the direct reports in their work. • Frequently review work progress and performance of direct reports. • Respond in a timely manner to individual performance challenges and do not let performance challenges escalate.
Select team members	• Select qualified team members who contribute well to overall team performance. • Make the tough decisions and proactively replace team members who consistently fall short of delivering their objectives. • Select team members who hold potential to develop into other roles too.
Build the team	• Create an inclusive environment where teamwork and collaboration are valued. • Build a high level of engagement. • Create an open and trusting environment that encourages people to speak up.
Integrate upwards and sideways	• Keep the direct manager informed about progress. • In due course share anticipated obstacles. • Proactively coordinate work with relevant colleagues.

Figure 8.2. Leadership Portrait for Leaders-of-Others (2 of 2).
Source: Copyright Leadership Pipeline Institute.

the minute after they are completed. With the Leadership Portrait in place, you can pinpoint development areas and you can follow up on whether they have been achieved.

The transition triad—work values, time application, and skills—represent the input. There is work to be valued, there is time to be distributed, and there are skills to master. The transition triad plays a key role in the development of leaders. For example, let's say you ask yourself questions such as "What is standing in the way of this leader's performance?" or "How can I help the leader perform even better?" or "Why has this leader not created development plans for their direct reports?" In the most common scenarios, the leader lacks appropriate work values, though ineffective time management and insufficient skills can play a part as well. Accordingly, you need to design your leadership development on the entire transition triad and not just the skills.

When assessing the potential of a leader-of-others moving into a leader-of-leaders role, start by assessing whether the leader in question has fully transitioned into their leader-of-others role. If yes, then you need to compare the leader-of-others portrait with the leader-of-leaders portrait and ask yourself, "Has the leader-of-others demonstrated anything on the job that indicates they are ready for the leader-of-leaders role?" "Have they demonstrated potential in relation to the required work values and skills? In the absence of Leadership Portraits, you will most often find that discussions on leadership potential become abstract and lack facts. *Personal biases start to carry too much significance.* Promoting people is a business decision. It is like any other investment decision. Applied the right way, the Leadership Portraits lead you to the facts you need. It is the process used in any business decision and it significantly increases the level of certainty in promotions.

When producing Leadership Portraits, it is important that they indeed become *your* Leadership Portraits. You might notice that we have left empty space in the boxes listing **Work Values**, **Time Application**, and **Skills**. We invite you to carefully consider if there are additional critical elements that should be included. Also, some organizations end up replacing **Skills** with **Competencies** in order to include their competency model as part of the Leadership Portrait. Some organizations replace **Work Values** with **Mindset** out of concern that people won't instantly understand the expression **Work Values**. Though the two words don't have identical meanings, it's more important to use the terminology that resonates best within the organization.

In order for the job-to-be-done details to be useful in your business, you'll likely want to adjust them for the different leadership roles/layers you apply them to. For example, it might be appropriate to add **Production Results**.

As for **The Work** column of Figure 8.2, it is important to include only real leadership work that is to be carried out by the leadership role in question. This is not a time for wishful thinking about leadership—just stick to actual work. Also, you may want to change the terminology; some prefer *empower*, and others prefer *delegate*. That is all up to you. If you have to translate the model into different languages, you may also want to take into consideration what words are easier to translate. You may also want to add an additional area of work relevant to your leaders-of-others roles. We do, however, urge you to prioritize and not design a model with many more work areas. Instead, use the model to help leaders focus on what is really important in their role.

The **Required Activities** column in Figure 8.2 is used to make the model hands-on and easy to use for leaders at all levels. This column answers questions such as "What does it mean to set direction, empower, and build the team? It is important to be very descriptive. This is where you explain what it is the leaders need to do on the job. You may want to add more statements. You may also want to rephrase some statements or use a different term—under "Empower," some organizations operate with "Check-in" sessions and others operate with "One-on-one" sessions, though the purpose and content of the conversation is the same. The statements overall should also capture your company culture. There are many different ways of saying the same thing, and you may be driving a special people agenda that requires that you strengthen some of the statements or repeat certain underlying agendas across the statements.

Choosing the Implementation Degree

We usually experience two different approaches to the implementation of the Leadership Pipeline concept:

- Full-scale implementation

- Partial implementation

The upsides of doing a full-scale implementation across the company are as follows:

- You get the dimensions and performance expectations defined so they are used everywhere.

- You get an upfront full alignment with other corporate-wide people, tools, and processes.

- You avoid having different leadership models dominating different parts of the organization.

These upsides are quite obvious and can hardly surprise anyone. What is less obvious is that you can also do a partial implementation or sequential implementation if that is easier to sell.

Partial implementation usually comes in two different shades. Some organizations start by implementing the model for all leadership layers within one distinct part of the organization, for example, one function or one business unit or one geographical area. Others have started with one leadership layer such as leaders-of-others or they start with top 100 executives as part of an executive development program or a succession planning process.

One of the most frequent reasons for partial implementation is that one unit believes it extremely important to get started quickly and they have the resources to do so. Their corporate human resources function does not have the resources and are busy with other corporate initiatives. Another reason for partial implementation is that a large company wants to pilot the solution in one unit to see how it works before rolling it out to the rest of the organization.

There are multiple upsides to a partial implementation strategy. First of all, you can move faster by identifying one organizational unit for whom this is a critical initiative. It also allows you to test different tools and processes before going full scale. From a change management perspective, you will be able to generate visible short-term wins and strong anecdotal success stories.

As always, if the project is not managed wisely, then the upsides can easily turn into downsides:

- The pilot unit insists on customizing the concept too much to their specific needs.

- Other units may feel alienated from the concept because they were not part of designing it.

- The short-term wins and anecdotal stories are too unit specific and hence not transferrable.

The conclusion is that if you do a partial implementation, you need to be certain that someone brings a corporate mindset to the project to ensure that the framework is designed in such a way that it can be a success for the pilot unit and later on can be used by the rest of the organization.

Whether the partial or the full-scale implementation is best for your organization depends entirely on your starting point. But you can rest assured that both strategies can lead to the same results.

Situating the Leadership Pipeline Framework

This second phase of implementation concerns several different questions that you'll need to ask about your particular situation.

How Does the Framework Fit with Our Corporate Title Structure?

Most companies operate with an internal title structure and some have external structures for marketing or public relations purposes. We see multiple title structures in many businesses. The purpose is often the same: identifying authority and/or status. Titles usually convey the hierarchical structure and say little about the actual role people are in. Some organizations have a mixture of hierarchy and roles built into the title structure. For instance, we see companies with country-based organizations where the head of a country is a business leader, and they are named *managing directors*. In manufacturing companies, we also see an example of this. A head of a production site may be named *production director*.

But what all the title approaches have in common is that they are typically designed top-down with a focus on leadership positions, and they are aligned with corporate hierarchy rather than the actual leadership work to be done. This means that in one company you can easily have managers and leaders-of-others with such different titles as supervisor, manager, director, or vice president. The titles are not attached to the work; they are attached to the hierarchical position of the role. Most corporate titles make perfect sense and fulfill an important role for the company.

However, this hierarchical title system does not work well as the baseline for leadership development, performance assessment, succession planning, and similar people processes. A title does not define the job to be done—the role does.

But implementing the Leadership Pipeline principles results in a work-based system for selecting, developing, and assessing leadership. It does not mean that you cannot have a title structure based on hierarchy. You need them both and implemented the right way to coexist well in any organization.

How Does the Framework Fit with Our Job Classification Systems?

There are many good reasons for applying job classification systems. Most companies use one for salary benchmarks and some companies also use it to build a corporate title structure, as we discussed previously. Generic job classification systems can help organizations make sense of salaries and titles across functions, business units, and geographies. However, it is not going to help you do succession planning, performance assessment, or the development of leaders. To be successful in these areas in relation to specialists, you need to take the approach provided by the Specialist Pipeline framework. Consider the following example.

Case study

A large energy company was represented in multiple business ventures, such as oil and gas production, building and managing wind farms, energy trading, and a couple of other business areas. Each business was organized as a self-sustainable business unit—though supported by the same group functions, such as finance, human resources, procurement, communication, and legal.

The business units were different in size and maturity. The biggest business unit counted for 40% of the gross income. Other business units counted for 30%, 15%, and 10%, leaving 5% to some small scale-up business units.

Using this case study as an example, let's examine the challenges you'd face if you used the job classification system without combining it with a role-based Leadership Pipeline approach.

The major business unit in the case company had a much bigger impact on overall company results compared to the smaller business units. Accordingly, the job classification of the business leader and probably the function leaders in the bigger business unit were greater than the job classes for similar roles in the smaller business units. However, the job to be done for a business leader or for a function leader remains the same regardless of the size of the business unit; these leaders are held accountable for the same type of leadership *work*. The point is that their development plans must focus on developing them for function leader and business leader *roles*.

You may also have leaders-of-leaders in the larger business unit whose job has a higher classification than the function leader role in the smaller business unit. Nevertheless, it is still a leader-of-leaders role.

The point is not that you shouldn't be using a job classification system. As we mentioned previously, this type of system certainly is required. However, when it comes to designing your Leadership Pipeline, the job classification system doesn't help. The trick to success is to allow the two systems to coexist.

How Does the Leadership Pipeline Framework Tie into Existing Skills or Competency Models?

We have come across many different types of leadership competency models. Some are simple models with five or seven high-a level competencies and some are more comprehensive models with a large number of competencies and multiple dimensions. They were being used for assessment, development, recruitment, succession planning, and other similar functions. We are usually invited in because the competency models weren't doing enough.

As you reflect on the Leadership Portrait concept you will realize why operating with leadership competency models as the backbone of leadership assessment, leadership development, and succession planning is destined to fail. Leadership competencies are input, but just one input out of three we know to be important. They don't include time application, they don't include work values, and they aren't differentiated by layer. The business leader and the call center supervisor use the same competencies. They also lack direct connection to the job to be done, so it is difficult to measure their effectiveness. Competency models have their merits, but not as a backbone system or an overall leadership framework.

When assessing performance of leaders and leadership quality, you need to look at the output. For example:

- What is the leader delivering?

- Is the leader delegating?

- Is the leader selecting for leadership?

- Is the leader developing the functional strategy?

Leadership performance should be assessed against the details of the job to be done. It is good to have competencies, but they are less important if you can't connect them to results.

Leaders must develop toward performing better in the current or future job to be done. It may be that the leader needs to build new skills/competencies. That leader also needs to build new work values and to ensure they efficiently prioritize their time. Competencies aren't comprehensive enough to stand alone, especially at the leader-of-others and leader-of-leaders levels. It's the work values that most commonly derail leaders at these levels. In fact, we meet many leaders who indeed have the competencies/ skills but they just don't apply them, simply because they don't value leadership work the same way as individual contributor work so they spend their time as an individual contributor.

Also, most competency models we come across are not differentiated by layer/role. In models we have seen with seven or so competencies, only two of the competencies are relevant to the executive level, and just a few to frontline managers. But, more important, they simply don't help leaders understand what to deliver in everyday life, and they don't help leaders-of-leaders understand what they should hold other leaders accountable for.

However, in many cases the competency models have been carefully developed, with executive involvement and at a significant cost. Consequently, they are there to stay. Accordingly, the key to success is making the existing competence coexist rather than compete with the Leadership Pipeline framework.

For the simple models with five or seven high-level leadership competencies, this is done by defining the competencies as the collective leadership aspiration for the organization and then apply the Leadership Portraits as the day-to-day operational tool.

For the more comprehensive models, this is done by taking the detailed competencies and including them under "Skills" in the transition triad. Alternatively, rename "Skills" to "Competencies" and combine them under that label.

Simply put, the value of competencies to the business is hard to measure. The behavior they suggest isn't meaningful unless it can be tied directly to results. The competencies may help to create a favorable work environment but they don't deliver results.

9

Tips for Fine-Tuning
the Implementation

The previous chapter spelled out some basics of how to implement the Leadership Pipeline. Many companies have implemented it successfully and, without exception, are glad they did. During the process there are many choices for business leaders and HR to make, all of which are influenced by both the size of the company and the state of leadership development. Many of these companies have shared their experiences with us; from their feedback, and our own, we've learned what tends to work and what doesn't. This chapter relays some tips to help implementation go smoothly.

But before we share those tips we'd like to say a few things. First, note that implementation may mean fixing the pipeline you already have. It is highly likely that you already have some version of a leadership pipeline. Some differentiation between layers already exists, certainly for decision-making, hiring, and spending money.

Second, it can be very helpful to consider how well your established pipeline is serving you. To follow are just a few signs that your leadership pipeline is broken:

- If the specialist/professional population in your organization isn't sure where to look for direction, your leadership pipeline is broken.

- If you are having trouble developing enough leaders, your leadership pipeline is broken.

- If there are bottlenecks where work flow gets stuck, your leadership pipeline is broken.

- If people are quitting due to a lack of engagement or don't feel there is purpose to their work, your leadership pipeline is broken.

- If the learning from your leadership development programs doesn't translate to the workplace, your leadership pipeline is broken.

And third, what's important is to realize that it just isn't possible to develop leaders properly without first clearly differentiating the definitions of the various layers. These definitions must be understood, practiced, and measured. When we say "implement the leadership pipeline" we mean defining the differences between layers, measuring leadership performance, and developing leadership capability by using these definitions consistently across the organization. And note: we're not talking about the technical or operational aspects of roles such as market share percentage or sales dollar targets. We're talking about planning requirements (strategic versus operational, long term versus short term); you add the subjects to be addressed. Differentiating the definitions of the various layers is so important it's the first item of the first list.

Universal Tips

Some implementation tips seem to apply everywhere. These are ideas that form the foundation, and so we conclude that everyone should consider using them.

For Each Layer, Clarify the Differentiation in Accountability Between Layers/Roles

Start by focusing on the leaders-of-others and the leaders-of-leaders. In our experience, significant breakage occurs at both of these levels. In any event those layers contain most of your leadership positions. To get a full understanding of where things stand, conduct several interviews with leaders-of-others and leaders-of-leaders—about six interviews with each layer is sufficient. Call these *work interviews* and clarify that the discussion is not about performance—it's about getting role clarity. Make sure the person being interviewed doesn't feel judged—if they do, you won't get accurate responses.

Ask them questions like these:

- What results are you supposed to deliver?

- What tasks do you perform to deliver those results?

- In increments of 5%, where does your time go?

- Where would you like to spend more time? Less time?

- What decisions do you make? Where would you like more authority?

- What development do you think you need?

Aggregate the data by question and compare it to the models in appropriate chapters. Map out the differences. Be sure to use the language of your business, not ours. Then, review it with next level up for validation. Conduct a feedback session focused on the work, *not on performance*. The point is to get understanding of and commitment *to* needed leadership work.[1]

Note: You may be shocked, as we have been, to see how much leading others' work is being done by leaders-of-leaders. Responses from those leading others will probably reveal that they are doing way too much leading-self work.

Keep Things Simple

There is a (natural?) tendency to create programs or start change initiatives when implementing something new. Building your leadership pipeline is closer to being the exact opposite of a program, so don't call it a program. It is about going back to fundamentals, that is, getting the basic leadership work done. The objective is to have those in leadership roles focus more on the leadership work in order to make the business work better. Allocating appropriate time to planning, hiring, assigning work, monitoring progress, giving feedback, coaching, and allocating rewards is the objective. It is no more complicated than that. Both business performance and leadership performance should improve together. It is likely some training will be needed to get everyone up to an appropriate standard.[2]

Tips for Business Leaders

Most business leaders want to have confidence that their organization can deliver the right products at the right time, cost, and quality. They are highly dependent on leaders-of-leaders and leaders-of-others to deliver through their teams, that is, design the product, build the product, sell the product, and deliver

---

[1] For a more complete treatment of this subject, see *The Performance Pipeline* by Stephen Drotter (Jossey-Bass, 2011).

[2] The Leadership Pipeline Institute offers courses for leading others, leading leaders, and function leaders.

the product. The function leaders should be doing more strategic work. It is in their best interest to build the pipeline.

Inspire Leadership Effort at the Lower Layers

Direct communication, face-to-face, on a regular basis is required. It doesn't have to be frequent but it should be regular. Meetings with groups or individuals at these two layers to convey your expectations and hear their concerns should be a building block for delivering to customers. Explain what you want them to work on, such as engagement, coaching, development, feedback, and support for the leading-self population. Explaining the difference in roles of leaders-of-leaders and leaders-of-others will enhance clarity. Meet with all the leaders-of-others and leaders-of-leaders; don't leave anyone out. Connect their leadership work to the success of the business. Allow time for questions. Several of our customers have printed the role definitions on large sheets of paper and posted them on the wall in offices, conference rooms, and factories.

Make a Full and Flowing Leadership Pipeline Part of Your Business Strategy

It is well established that effective leadership is a source of competitive advantage. It is one of the very few sources of *sustained competitive advantage*. It is also well understood that the strength of your leadership is one of the strongest leading indicators of future business success. If your cadre of leaders can attract, retain, develop, and deploy people better than competitors, you will execute better than competitors and win in the marketplace on a sustained basis. In most business strategies leadership strength isn't addressed, so jump out ahead.

Run a Comprehensive Succession Planning Process

If you want the business effectiveness that leadership strength can deliver, you have to plan it, make decisions, invest your time and money, and take some risks. Succession planning is the vehicle for doing that work. Succession planning isn't an HR program, it is a business process. Its object is to prepare your business for its likely future. HR can design your succession planning process and engineer it, but you have to operate it.

Tips for HR Leaders

It may seem that building the leadership pipeline is "HR's job." Certainly HR has a major role to play. Although they are not accountable for the performance of individual leaders, they have accountability for the collective performance of all leaders. Programs, processes, courses, coaching, rewards, and so on then enable leadership performance. A responsibility of this size needs to be understood and accepted by HR. Design of the architecture that enables leadership performance and development is where it starts. Engineering the programs to support individual leaders' success is also a major accountability. This accountability won't be fulfilled if HR waits to be asked. They don't need permission to do their job; they need courage.

Take a Step Back to Be Sure About What's Working and What Isn't

Jumping in with solutions before you can clearly articulate the problems and opportunities is foolhardy. There is a good deal of important information available.

Pay close attention to the traffic into HR. Consider the following:

- Why are they coming to HR?

- What are people (leaders and non-leaders) asking for?

- What problem are they presenting?

- Where are they placing the blame?

- What are the best performers asking for?

- What do the operating results tell you about what's working and what isn't?

- How well are those who were promoted to any leadership level making the transition?

- How well are external hires in leadership positions performing?

Formulate clear statements of the issues that need to be addressed. Consider every aspect and all programs as fair game for the solutions.

Connect All the Elements on the Human Side of Your Business

Your leadership pipeline can't be built or fixed with individual transactions. Hiring one good leader is useful but doesn't fix or build anything. Running one course, no matter how successful it was, won't build a better pipeline. We would like to tell you to just read our books or take our courses and all will be well. It is much more important to look at these issues:

- **Recruiting and selection specifications.** Are you hiring for leadership positions based on technical skills or leadership potential?

- **Your succession planning process.** Do those identified for promotion succeed after they are promoted?

- **The collection of courses you run or recommend.** Are they generic or specific? What is being applied at work?

- **Performance criteria used for rewards and promotions.** Are poor leaders given raises and bonuses?

- **Instructions given to external coaches.** Are they
  made aware of your standards and expectations for
  leaders or are they just using their own?

- **Career planning and management.** What are interested
  employees told about moving into leadership roles?
  What are they told about moving up to bigger
  leadership roles?

All of these elements should work together toward the same
end. The best way to connect them is by using the same standard.
We suggested as our first tip that definitions be created to clearly
define the differences between layers. Those templates can be the
standards used for recruiting, promotions, rewards, training programs, and so on. This simple step—using the same standard for
all transactions—will start you on your way to a leadership pipeline
that is full and flowing. It is important to note that job-specific
requirements can and should be added to the templates for various
transactions, such as operational goals for rewards. Our main point
is the same specific standard should be the core used in all catego-
ries of judgment.

Tips for HR Business Partners

HR business partners are the boots on the ground for building a
Leadership Pipeline. Interactions with various layers, observing
leaders in action, hearing how leaders are received by those reporting to them, and conversing with unhappy employees are all
sources of information about how leaders are leading. That information is vital for decision-making about current and future
leaders. This real-time view from underneath the organization
structure on how leaders are performing is unique and invaluable.
It deserves attention and should lead to meaningful action.

Consolidate What You See, Hear, and Experience About the Leaders You Support

On a daily basis—preferably, or at least weekly—take stock of what you have learned about the leaders you support. It will help you in providing feedback and suggestions to those leaders and is an important part of better developing leaders. *HR business partners should have well-founded opinions about the performance and potential of leaders in the organization they support.* This has nothing to do with "king-making" or "spying." The purpose is to support current performance and development. Answering these questions will help:

- What have I learned about leader X this week?

- Is this part of a pattern or just a one-time occurrence?

- How, exactly, should I convey this so it will be helpful and constructive?

- Who else should know and when?

There isn't anything unusual about doing this. Many leaders, especially the good ones, ask for this feedback. The leadership development organization needs to hear about any patterns that emerge, such as several leaders with the same problem. A course may be a better way to achieve improvement.

Provide Support for Leaders Making Transitions

In our experience, every leader benefits from some early support when making the transition to a new leadership position. Hardly any get that support. HR business partners are positioned to be helpful. One myth that needs to be exposed and eliminated is "let new leaders settle in for a few weeks and then let's see how they are doing." The opposite has proven to be a better approach. Left to fend for themselves, leaders will naturally stick with doing what has made them successful in their previous job. The new role may not be entirely clear to them.

Start by discussing the specifics of the new layer. Use the leadership portraits you have developed or the appropriate chapter from this book with a focus on the transition required in work values, time application, and skills. Pay particular attention to establishing the new mindset.

Finding meaning in the new role is the next step. Use the template for the job to be done. Add the specific or unique requirements for this particular role in your company. Meaning will come from understanding the value this position will add.

Some change in self-image is probably required. For a new leader-of-others the change is substantial. They were one of the gang—now they're the leader of the gang. The gang will be looking for direction, support, engagement, career advice, coaching, and much more. Pretending to still be one of them is destructive. The HR business partner should help this new leader prepare for these new conversations. New leaders must see themselves as the person who will fill those needs. Being more thoughtful and knowledgeable when engaging with the old gang changes the conversation. Thinking this through before engaging with the old gang is critical and the HR business partner makes that thinking happen. The gang needs to see the new leader as someone they can trust and count on. The first meeting with them can't be the same old thing. They need to see their new leader as a leader.

Transition assistance usually takes more than one meeting. Planning for follow-up discussions is a normal part of the support. Having someone to talk with who isn't their boss usually makes them more willing to share their concerns and work at addressing them.

Dance with Whoever Wants to Dance

If the business has purposely set out to build its leadership pipeline, there should be acceptance for HR business partners to give feedback or help with leadership transitions. Not every leader will agree or make time for their HR business partner. It is safe to say some leaders do want help or advice in order to improve or be more promotable. Start with them. Waiting for a corporate edict or for the business leader to launch an initiative isn't necessary. Many leaders want to be the best they can be. Dance with them. They will tell their friends, who will then want to dance. Others will see you dancing and ask to join in. This grassroots approach has been successful in many businesses.

Things Not to Do—By Anyone

Some implementation activities are mistakes that don't fall directly to any person or part of the organization. General awareness should suffice as tips.

Don't Wait for an Edict

Success is possible no matter where you start. Edicts aren't really necessary. We have worked with companies and businesses that have started at the level of CEO or at a function leader level or at the level of a unit within operations. All have been successful. What matters most is to start where you can.

Don't Confuse Your Title with Your Role

Titles convey status, not necessarily the job to be done. They are used quite differently from company to company. Vice presidents can have no direct reports and are therefore leading themselves. Leaders without officer titles can have thousands of people in the organization they run. We are focused on the job to be done. Look past the status title when deciding how to include someone in the leadership pipeline. It is important to note that some critical positions in a corporate staff without direct reports may have enterprise-wide responsibilities so we think of them as function or sub-function leaders.

Don't Arbitrarily Use the Language in This Book

The language we've used in this book, such as *leader* or *function* or *enterprise*, may not fit your organization. You're free to use our language if it helps, but if there might be any confusion, we encourage you to use your own terminology. Designate the layers or roles in a way that suits your situation. All that really matters is having consistent language to differentiate the accountability.

Tips for Unclogging the Pipeline

You have given the implementation your best effort but you aren't getting enough progress. It is highly likely that your leadership pipeline is *clogged*. Something more drastic should be considered in order to free up the flow. Here are some choices.

Return to Their Previous Specialist or Professional Role Those Leaders Who Won't Make Time For or Can't Do Leadership Work

Not everyone is cut out for leadership work. Not every person in a leadership role is there by choice. Some people try leadership but after a while find it isn't what they expected or want. Leaving people in leadership roles who don't want to be there or shouldn't be there clogs your leadership pipeline. It is common for these to be performing poorly. The people who work for them are getting shortchanged on coaching, feedback, career planning, and engagement, among other things. No one is happy or, ultimately, productive. When calculating the benefit to the individuals, the leader in question, and the company, this is a lose-lose-lose proposition. A thorough discussion with that leader is usually required before any reassignment is made. Presumably the leader in question was effective in a leading-self position, which was the reason for the promotion to leading others. Returning to that role is a win-win for that person and the company. It may be a win for the employees if they end up with a better, more willing leader. It is common for businesses to wait too long before taking any action on ineffective leaders. Waiting and tolerating less than satisfactory performance or unhappy leaders lowers the standards for leadership and makes it difficult to improve your leadership pipeline.

Increase the Span-of-Control to Reduce Role Confusion

A frequent objection to reassigning leaders to specialist/professional positions is there won't be enough replacements. Consider the spans of control that are in place. Leaders-of-others with five or fewer direct reports aren't getting a taste of real leadership work. Doing lots of technical work is necessary to fill their day. The design of their job forces them to stay in the technical work. In our experience, the appropriate span of control for proper development of leaders is 10 to 30. The upper end of this range is common in large production organizations such as call centers and some retail stores. Leadership work can fill most of their day. The lower end is for technical and professional work where tough technical problems must be solved. Spans of less than five should be reserved for leading-edge technology or big-ticket selling.

Final Note

We hope you found this chapter helpful. We'd also be very interested in hearing how you handle all this in your organization. Send one of us an email; our addresses are in the Welcome section.

10

Meaningful Dialogues for Performance, Engagement, and Retention

"Nobody likes performance reviews; get rid of them!" "Times are tough; we don't have any budget for development!" "I am much too busy to coach anyone." If this is what you and others in your organization are thinking, think again. Poor retention, lack of engagement, quiet quitting, burnout, and many other problems of the moment arise from this kind of organizational thinking. Once employees sense they're not valued—by the company in general or by their leaders in particular—they're likely to quit and leave, or quit and stay, or use social media to express their opinion of the company. We can't stress this enough: you will see no performance improvement and no development without meaningfully engaging with your employees.

Some organizations have abandoned performance scores, and others still use them. Some organizations apply structured semiannual performance conversations; others apply continuous performance conversations. One structure is not better than the other, and neither will address the problems listed previously. The only way to address these problems is by regularly conducting meaningful performance and development dialogues at all levels.

Current wisdom says leaders should address these problems by "having empathy," "listening more," "communicating more," "being transparent," "being authentic," and so on. Although any of these approaches will likely produce some temporary progress, they won't get at the core problem unless employees and leaders hear exactly why they are valued and why their work is important. So, let's talk about how, using the Leadership Pipeline.

In this chapter we will demonstrate how the Leadership Portraits will help you get to where you want to be. Further, we will introduce the Leadership Pipeline Performance Circles. Whether you like performance scoring systems or not, the circles will help all leaders when having a fact-based conversation about what success looks like in any given role—and to what extent the employee in question is filling out their role. Also, the performance circles will guide the dialogue straight from performance to development.

Where to Start

To help you get this important work right, we offer the following guidance from our years of experience.

Simultaneously manage both current and future performance by providing development. Working with employees to help them develop is one of the most powerful tools you have for strengthening retention.

Discuss each employee's performance and development with them regularly. The best feedback comes in the moment, not six months later—and regularly, not periodically.

Start where the employee is. Find out what they think about their performance, development needs, and potential before offering your judgment. Striving to build a bridge from their position to yours can help to clarify the path forward while avoiding potential conflict. (You'll also likely learn valuable information from these discussions.)

The most constructive feedback includes thoughtful answers to the following questions:

- "What is expected of me?"

- "How does my work fit into the business?"

- "How am I doing?"

- "Can I get some help with this work problem?"

- "Where can I get the development I need?"

- "How are you [their immediate manager] going to support me in my development?"

- "What is my likely future here?"

Answers to these questions must be included if the dialogue is to be effective. These seem to be universal problems. The first responsibility for every leader is to make sure their direct reports know and understand what is expected of them. The second is to make sure they know how they're doing. We have described this responsibility in previous chapters but from the leader's point of view. Now we want leaders to see it from the employee's point of view. If a leader isn't providing these answers, they are sowing the seeds of unrest—because here is where an employee's desire to leave their employer starts.

These questions are effective because they engage employees in meaningful dialogue. This dialogue, this one-on-one time *focused on their needs*, not the company's or the leader's needs, fundamentally demonstrates that the employee is valued. And because the answers to these questions may change as business activity unfolds, projects get completed, obstacles emerge, new goals are established, and so on, more dialogue will always be needed, which is why it's imperative that these discussions be conducted regularly.

Answering these questions is beneficial to the leader as well. The performance of both participants in these discussions will likely improve because the conversations offer greater clarity and focus for the employee and useful feedback for the leader. What's more, it's likely that the leaders have the same questions about their own situation.

Absent these discussions, any employee will feel undervalued or disconnected. They are likely to assume the worst, such as "My work isn't important," "I don't count," "I am not performing," "They are going to demote me," "I'm going to be let go." When employees feel disconnected or uncertain, their common responses are quiet quitting and searching for a new employer. Neither of these is good for business.

We have met many leaders who question our advice, believing that this guidance simply derives from the younger generation having too high expectations. However, these leaders are missing two key points:

- This is what leaders should do as leaders! If they are not inclined to offer this support, they'd be wise to instead step away from their leadership roles.

- Doing all this is not only of value to the employees. The performance of any leader equals the consolidated performance of their direct reports. So, why would they not help their direct reports understand what good performance looks like—and then help them get there?

What to Watch Out For

Not all performance shortfalls are the same; some are much bigger than others. Two important performance problems for leaders have a rippling effect on the people around them. They can't be overlooked or swept under the rug because their circle of influence can be quite large. And yet, they're also frequently missed.

Leaders Working at the Wrong Level

We've seen this happening in every company that has hired us: leaders doing work intended for their direct reports—because they haven't let go of the work they used to do. (Although this is most commonly observed at that leader-of-others level, it happens at all levels.)

This is the biggest mistake a leader can make. Everybody loses. That leader doesn't make the right contributions and doesn't grow professionally. The direct reports don't get to make the right contributions and don't grow professionally. They also don't get the management attention they need to feel engaged—which calls for that leader's manager needing to step in and do the work the leader should be doing, in addition to their own work. This a common cause of burnout.

If a leader or a group of leaders is working at the wrong leadership level, there is major repair work to do. Specifically, they must develop the appropriate work values, time application, and skills for their level in order to ensure appropriate job performance. Future performance and promotions are dependent on that development.

This is a challenging task for two reasons. First, in many organizations, role clarity for leadership work is minimal or absent. Although organizations may do a good job of defining financial and operational requirements, they often do a poor job of defining leadership requirements and differentiating them by leadership level. As a result, even individuals who want to improve their leadership performance have difficulty doing so because they aren't clear about what their targets should be.

Roles Remaining Undefined

Most companies fail to create Leadership Portraits that are differentiated by leadership level. In fact, Leadership Portraits tend to be nonexistent. Required performance tends to be financial and operational rather than a complete set of performance requirements that include leadership results. Consequently, it's difficult if not impossible to measure leadership results at any of the levels.

Think about how employees react to situations in which role requirements aren't clear and standards for what success looks like aren't in place. It is highly unlikely they will be dedicated and content with their situation. The world around them seems arbitrary, and they aren't getting the support they need from their leader. This lack of definition produces ambivalence and ambivalence paralyzes people at work.

The Leadership Pipeline provides a fast and effective way to improve role definition. In Chapter 8 we illustrated how you create Leadership Portraits for each leadership role based on the Leadership Pipeline model. You can sharpen role definition by comparing (1) what a leader *does* versus what is *required* in a given leadership role and (2) what the immediate manager and direct report do versus the Leadership Pipeline model. Because most development occurs on the job, it's important to establish the appropriate Leadership Portraits so a leader understands them and develops in the right direction.

Using Leadership Pipeline Performance Circles

Leadership portraits aren't theoretical concepts that are nice to think about but difficult to apply. The portraits we've defined and used in conjunction with the leadership pipeline are concrete and have enabled organizations to develop leaders at all levels with greater speed and effectiveness.

The problem with performance conversations tends to be in the eye of the beholder. If you take six leaders-of-leaders at six companies, they may all provide convincing arguments about what constitutes "doing a good job." As sincere as they may be in wanting to do this part of their job well, they probably all have very different ideas about what a good job is. Even if their roles have been clarified in terms of work values, time application, and skills, they may translate responsibilities into very different activities and results.

Well-defined Leadership Portraits, therefore, are crucial to achieving appropriate engagement. Without them, it's virtually impossible to convey leadership expectations and requirements. We've also created Leadership Pipeline Performance Circles to help users visualize current performance—including performance gaps and development opportunities—without using a scoring system. We've found this approach to be a much more motivating and nonthreatening way to conduct a performance conversation. In fact, the leader can ask direct reports themselves to fill in their own circles in advance based on the Leadership Portrait for their position.

Everything inside the circle is the responsibility of the individual who holds this job, and everything outside the circle is someone else's responsibility. Lines drawn inside the circle show the relative completion of a desired result. A full performer would therefore have a circle that looks like the left circle in Figure 10.1. This full-performance circle is the goal of development activities. On the right is the most common circle. It indicates that, although some performance dimensions are being met, others have not yet been met.

Next, consider the two circles in Figure 10.2. Note that though the left circle represents exceptional performance—the dotted

Figure 10.1. Two Portraits of Performance: (1) Full Performance and (2) Not-Yet-Full Performance.
Source: Drotter Human Resources, Inc.

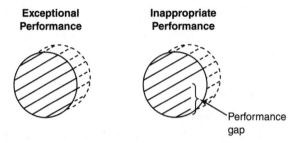

Figure 10.2. Two More Portraits of Performance: (3) Exceptional Performance and (4) Inappropriate Performance.
Source: Drotter Human Resources, Inc.

lines go beyond the circle, indicating performing above and beyond the requirements. It is performance that comes at a price. People with this profile feel as though they've outgrown their leadership role, and their ability to exceed the position requirements makes them restless and vulnerable to headhunters' calls. Serious dialogue about the future will be needed to retain this person.

The circle on the right is troubling. Those with this profile are often doing much more of things they like doing—as indicated by the dotted lines outside the main circle. But although they're reaching beyond their role, they're also not doing the work they should be doing—as indicated by the performance gap. Dialogue on role clarification will be needed to both rein in inappropriate performance and promote the proper attitude or understanding.

These four circles can be used to convey performance status to employees at all levels, helping them see where they're performing well and where they're coming up short. Figure 10.3 illustrates how to fill the leadership pipeline by using these circles as a developmental guide.

1. Appointment to a new leadership level will immediately create a performance gap because they haven't yet done the job. They have to learn the work values, time applications, and skills required for success at the new level.

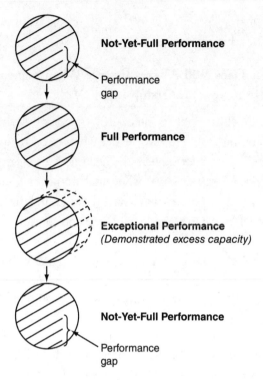

Figure 10.3. Using Performance Portraits to Define Development Needs.

Source: Drotter Human Resources, Inc.

Consequently, they are not immediately capable of delivering strong results in each key area.

2. Development should be directed toward closing the gap through coaching, training, and other means. Achieving full performance will usually take a little time and effort.

3. Once people reach full performance, test them to see whether they can handle additional responsibilities and demonstrate excess capacity.

4. Move exceptional performers to more challenging assignments or to the next leadership level. When they move to the next leadership level, expect another performance gap, which takes you back to step one.

This four-step process won't work unless you accept the following underlying premises.

Performance Gaps Will Always Emerge When Someone Is Appointed to a New Leadership Level

No matter how skilled or how successful someone is at the previous level, gaps are inevitable for any leader when entering a new leadership level. *The need for support and dialogue is strongest right here.* Once you accept these gaps as normal you can guide leaders through the learning process for closing them. Using the Leadership Pipeline model, you can provide guidance and training for the new level's work values, time application, and skills. At the same time, the leaders being developed must be informed and willing participants. This means they must be open to giving up the work, the methods, and the beliefs that made them successful in the past but aren't appropriate now.

Development Must Go on Until They Reach Full Performance

Partial performance is not sufficient. Everyone must accept full performance as the target. This acceptance is easier when organizations see full performance as a competitive advantage rather than some technical human resources concept. In effect, a company must be willing to make a strategic investment in developing leaders to the point of full performance in order to gain a competitive advantage.

Full Performers Should Be Tested for Excess Capacity—Then Promoted If They Demonstrate It

Excess capacity is a sign that someone is ready to take on more responsibility or move up a leadership level, and it should catalyze promotions. People can be tested by assigning work from the desk of someone on the leadership level above them and seeing which of the circles in Figure 10.4 emerges. If they can do it all, they are

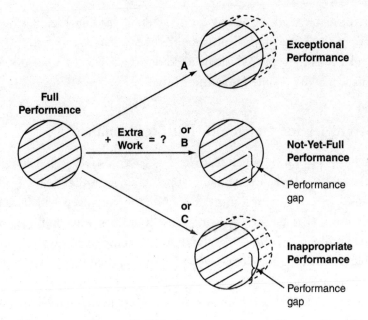

Figure 10.4. Testing Full Performers to Assess Future Capability.
Source: Drotter Human Resources, Inc.

ready for something bigger. If the testing doesn't work out so well, that leader should stay in the current position for the time being. If they were promoted, they wouldn't succeed—and it is almost impossible to reverse the process.

Figure 10.4 defines the most critical work for leaders. This approach requires frequent engagement. The frequency is usually reduced as results are delivered. Asking the person to draw their own performance profile is the best way to start the dialogue once the person settles in the role. Having them explain why the profile is the way it is offers important information for deciding on appropriate development and for planning support. Early signs of burnout and desire to leave can be addressed in the flow of work. Getting every employee up to speed as quickly as is practical is in the best interest of the employee, the leader, the business, and the customer. Leaders who say they are too busy to have these dialogues are probably working at the wrong level. Quiet quitting, burnout, looking to leave, and so on should never come as a surprise. If a leader tells their people they care about them but then fails to do this work, the people know the truth.

Strategies for Getting to Full Performance

A fully performing pipeline of leaders isn't possible if you simply rely on standard development approaches. Identifying the root causes of performance shortfalls, from the employee and in the situation, is crucial. By spotting these problems, you can pinpoint and eliminate pipeline clogs. Finding root causes requires considerable communication between the leader and their direct reports as well as situational analysis.

In a leader-led development culture, every leader in the business should be involved in finding and fixing performance shortfalls. If this seems like overkill, consider the analogy to a high-performance factory. In such a factory, input and output are tightly measured and performance is high because machine operators are trained and measured with great precision. Perfect operation is the goal. Technical support and training are used freely. Obviously, this analogy is somewhat flawed because the causes and effects of leadership problems can be much less visible than input and output in a factory. Still, exact training and measurement can greatly benefit any organization's leadership development, especially if full performance is the goal.

We've found that the following four leadership development strategies have proven to be very effective for companies attempting to improve the flow in their leadership pipeline.

Strategy 1: Start with the Manager, Not the Direct Report

When we run succession planning training programs, we ask the people enrolled in these programs to draw performance circles for their direct reports. We then ask them to list the reasons for any performance gaps; an incredible 75% of the reasons listed relate to the manager. Managers may be working at the wrong leadership level, for instance. Or they may be micromanaging or under-communicating. They may have made a hiring mistake. We're not saying the manager is the cause of all leadership performance problems. What we are saying is that the manager is the place to start if you want to increase full performance throughout the Leadership Pipeline.

Managers must ask themselves what they're doing (or not doing) that's impeding leadership development and performance of their direct reports. They must also ask themselves how they might change in order to promote better performance. You'll find the performance circles again useful in illustrating manager-caused performance problems (see Figure 10.5).

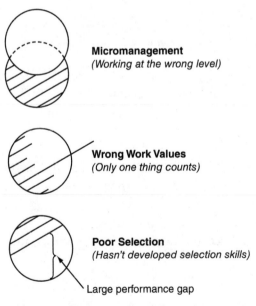

Figure 10.5. How Managers Cause Performance Gaps and Clog the Leadership Pipeline.
Source: Drotter Human Resources, Inc.

At the same time, you should also be aware that organizational factors—factors over which the manager has limited control—can result in performance gaps. The most commonly cited factors are the following:

- **Inappropriate organizational structure.** This is often due to unnecessary overlap—a matrix structure often produces this overlap.

- **Low-performance culture.** When "good enough" is good enough, poor performance is tolerated.

- **Poor job design.** Though a set of responsibilities has been identified and assigned, some may not be doable or even necessary.

- **Broken or nonexistent processes.** Full performance is rare when work doesn't flow or key people are left out of the processes that affect them.

- **Misallocation of power or authority.** The age-old issue here is responsibility without authority.

- **Improper staffing.** This occurs when the hiring process doesn't include astute analysis of job requirements and candidate specifications.

It is beyond critical to understand that the manager and the organization can cause poor performance, inadequate engagement, and declining retention.

Strategy 2: Search for Evidence of an Appropriate Values Shift

Most people make some short-term adjustments in their operating style, particularly when a job is new and not well understood. If you go simply on initial appearances, it may seem as though there has been a values shift. Don't rely on initial appearances.

Anyone can start new habits—it's maintaining them that matters. The leadership pipeline's viability is riding on a real value shift among many leaders. Behavior won't shift on a sustained basis without a real shift in work values and people won't take their leadership turns successfully.

The evidence of a values shift entails people willing to see their roles differently. They must be willing to reallocate their time, change the way they attack problems (or change which aspect of the problem they tackle personally), and accept new skill-building requirements. Mere verbalization of new values is insufficient.

People can talk all they want about being willing to give their direct reports more autonomy or becoming more of an integrator rather than an implementor, but unless there is tangible evidence of a sustained shift in behaviors, the values probably haven't changed. The next sections describe how to gather the necessary evidence.

Ask the Leader's Direct Reports

The best evidence about how leaders are leading comes from the "followers." There are several important reasons for talking to those who are two layers down, including validating succession plans, evaluating the distribution of rewards, and improving engagement and retention. Ask a few simple questions:

- How is the job going?

- What helps you get your job done?

- What interferes with your performance?

- How do you feel about this company?

- How do you see your future?

Asking employees two layers down from you to specifically evaluate their manager may well cause more problems than it solves.

If the manager is helping or getting in the way, these kinds of open-ended questions will give you the answers you need to know.

Conduct a "Lessons Learned" Discussion After Successes and Failures

As we've emphasized, verbalizing values is insufficient; nevertheless, what people say about their actions and behaviors can be telling. Ask questions after both successes and failures. For instance, after an employee fails to complete a project on time, ask, "What have we learned about our ability to meet deadlines?" "What do you think we should do?" If they start talking about how they didn't have the time—and their leadership level demands that they give their people authority to achieve assignments on their own—it's clear that a value shift hasn't taken place.

Examine Leaders' Calendars

Their calendars reveal priorities and time allocation, which in turn reveal values. If the calendar is filled with meetings, determine what the purpose of these meetings was, what decisions were made, and who made them. Were the types of meetings and decisions appropriate to the leadership level? Or was the leader spending time on activities better left to direct reports?

Listen Carefully to How Leaders Evaluate Direct Reports

If someone is fixated on one performance dimension—operating results, for instance—then it's clear what this leader values. Though all leaders should value all performance dimensions, there are particular value shifts that must be made at each leadership level, and when leaders focus exclusively on a particular dimension, it can indicate that they're stuck at a lower level.

Look at Plans Leaders Submit from a Values Standpoint

Plans often reveal what leaders value most. Look for what is most thoughtfully discussed in the plan or where the greatest amount of space and effort have been devoted. These points of emphasis are clues to values. In some cases, the plans themselves are inadequate—they demonstrate unclear thinking or erroneous assumptions—thus indicating this person doesn't value planning, which of course is an important aspect of leadership at all levels. It could be a skill problem, but if they valued planning, they would get help to ensure that a plan was produced.

Strategy 3: Support Leaders in Their Transition

As discussed in previous chapters, moving from one leadership role to another is a big event that requires a significant transition. Organizations need to make this visible to leaders. Otherwise, the transition is easily ignored or only understood at an intellectual level.

One way to support leaders making the transition successfully is implementing an onboarding process for each of the leadership roles. The process could be a six-month process in which you support the recently promoted leader in a structured way to understand and appreciate their new role. You may use various onboarding tools and systems, but most important for success is that the immediate manager of the recently promoted leader engages in conversations about expected leadership results in this role and how the immediate manager going to support the leader in stepping into the role.

A supplementary way of supporting the recently promoted leader is by designing action-learning, leadership-transition programs. These programs must equally focus on work values, time application, and skills. By *action learning* we mean that during the program the participants work on getting their own leadership work done; we're not referring to programs with simulations, artificial assignments, or theoretical lectures.

Strategy 4: Address Inappropriate Performance Immediately

Leadership pipelines clog when performance gaps are allowed to exist for lengthy periods. Not addressing these gaps immediately lets everyone know that the organization doesn't deem leadership passages particularly important. When leaders are allowed to operate below their appropriate leadership levels with impunity, it has a contagious impact on the entire leadership culture. (See Figure 10.6.)

As an example, if a leader-of-leaders steps down and takes on part of the leadership role of their direct reports—who are leaders-of-others—then the leaders-of-others are leaders in name only. The consequences of this are multiple:

- The leaders-of-others get the wrong picture of what it means to be a leader-of-others. They easily bring that misconception with them if one day they are promoted. And their direct reports will then suffer the same way.

- If the leader-of-leaders is not doing their job, there is only one person to cover the gaps and that is their immediate manager. This way, the immediate manager is partly dragged down to a lower leadership role.

- In connection with succession planning, we discuss the promotion of a leader-of-others to a leader-of-leaders role. We may believe that the person in question has been performing well in a leader-of-others role for five years. But in reality, they have never really been in a leader-of-others role because their direct manager was doing part of their job. On any leadership level, this behavior should be unacceptable, identified early, and remedied. The goal of the remedy should be to

Figure 10.6. The Inappropriate Performance Circle.
Source: Drotter Human Resources, Inc.

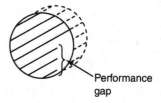

Performance gap

eliminate performance outside the defined leadership role and to encourage acceptance of the required leadership role. Then performance improvement should be pursued.

The Retention-Development Connection

The war for talent is not just a recruiting problem. Retention is becoming an increasingly significant concern of just about every organization as other companies lure talent, as technical skills are in increasingly short supply, and as employee attitudes about work and careers shift. Retention can be a salary and career advancement issue; it also can be closely linked to an organization's leadership development efforts. We've found that a strong development program that prepares people for full performance at all levels is an incentive for staying with an organization. People tend to stay where they can be successful, learn, and grow. Development requires strong engagement:

- Development is a very personal matter. It demonstrates that an organization cares for individual leaders and their success, regardless of whether they're first-time leaders or business leaders.

- Learning and growth are rewarding, desired feelings. In today's business climate, most people don't want to plateau and stagnate; they realize that feeling comfortable and secure is no longer the goal. People at all levels want faster movement. Learning and personal growth attract ambitious, talented leaders.

- Development is a particularly significant kind of engagement. Leaders who are in a development process or program get valuable feedback, often with personalized attention.

- Development is the ultimate perk. It can't be taken back once given, and it leads to other benefits.

In addition, the lack of a sound development program creates retention problems of another sort. Poorly developed leaders invariably impede the development of their direct reports by doing their work for them, modeling the wrong values, and so on. Frustrated, many of these direct reports leave the organization—especially the most talented among them, who are anxious to develop new leadership skills.

Of course, not just any leadership development program will be a good retention tool. In fact, any program that ignores these five leadership passages will drive people from the company because their development expectations won't be met. When organizations help leaders move from performance gaps at a given level to full or exceptional performance, they increase the odds that these leaders will stay in the pipeline.

11

How the Leadership Pipeline Model Is Applied to Unique Roles

Over the last ten years or so there has been a noticeable increase in the use of matrices, agile teams, flatter structures, rapidly evolving roles, and increased delegation of authority to enable knowledge workers to adapt quickly to changing requirements. Removing bureaucracy, increasing decision-making authority, shortening communication lines, improving resource utilization, and using multifunctional teams have all become common objectives.

All these structures affect leadership roles. That means a person can be a team leader on one day and a team member on the next. Moving from leading a team of people from the same function one day to leading a multifunctional team the next is an accepted practice. Sharing authority and accountability with other leaders from other organizations requires compromise and flexibility that's never been required before.

In the slipstream of these reorganizations, businesses have realized they need to formalize new types of leadership roles. The clarity and development needs related to the work values, time application, and skills encapsulated in the Leadership Pipeline model are just as critical in these alternative organizational structures—but some companies have struggled in transferring the Leadership Pipeline concepts from the traditional organizational structures into the new structures.

If this scenario captures your current situation, we have two points of good news for you. One, every leadership role can be accounted for with the Leadership Pipeline model. And two, to address this challenge, in this chapter we offer guidance for how to implement the Leadership Pipeline framework in several variations of organizational structures, both new and old, that have proven challenging for some companies. And though the leadership roles addressed in this chapter are just a few examples, we hope they can help you implement whatever roles you need to address.

When applying the Leadership Pipeline model, we need to keep the following sequence in mind:

- Map the leadership roles in scope.

- Define the job to be done for each role.

- Define the required work values, time application, and skills for each role.

Note: the roles we describe in this chapter vary quite a bit in definition, substance, and scope from one company to another. Accordingly, we can't provide a full description of the job to be done, nor a full set of work values, time application, and skills as we did with the core roles in Chapters 3 through 7. But we will highlight the core of the job to be done and describe some key work values and skills that are different from the basic model. We trust this can help you design the Leadership Portrait specific to the roles within your organization.

Project Leader

In order to deliver a large or complex product, some organizations ask people from various functions to work together exclusively on one deliverable. Those people report—usually temporarily—to a leader who has overall responsibility for producing the deliverable on time, on budget, and with the appropriate quality. Until the deliverable is complete, the team members involved may feel the pull of reporting simultaneously to two leaders—who may have very different agendas. For example, the function leader might want to pull their people off the project work to attend an important technical meeting.

There are also businesses that consistently use the project organization as their main operation model; construction, aerospace, and investment banking are just a few examples.

Case study

We were invited to speak to the top 60 managers in a large international company in the energy industry. Their main business centered on large-assets projects typically running over three to four years from greenfield to being operational. The company was organized as a project organization where 80% of all employees were engaged in projects at any given time. They had a typical organizational setup with line functions and a project organization. Employees reported to their function leader and their project leader.

The company had trouble retaining frontline specialists and project managers. One of the statements they frequently heard in resignation interviews was "In principle, I have two managers: my line manager and my project manager. But in reality, I don't feel I have any manager taking care of me. My line manager doesn't know what's going on because I work 95% of my time on projects, and my project manager only cares about getting the project finalized—not about my development or my career."

We were invited to speak because they found the Leadership Pipeline model intriguing but didn't think it could work in a project organization with project managers

> and project directors who are not traditional leaders-of-others and leaders-of-leaders. We asked the managers, "What is the difference between the line manager role and the project manager role?" They all quickly agreed that "the line manager secures the people resources, and the project manager uses the people resources."

The basic division of work between the line manager and the project manager was that the line manager was responsible for selecting people externally, deploying people internally, conducting performance reviews, and developing the employees. The project manager was then supposed to execute the project with the people assigned to them. This is a setup we see in most project organizations. And, given that division of work, the managers were correct—the Leadership Pipeline model will help neither the line manager nor the project manager. This is because, in this sort of setup, line manager work is about leadership and project manager work is about task management. However, the existing definition of "who does what"—line manager versus project manager—was what caused all their challenges.

Because we subscribe to the 70–20–10 rule of development—70% challenging assignments, 20% developmental relationships, and 10% coursework—we believe most development should take place on the job. But how is the line manager supposed to develop their direct reports on the job when they don't see them on the job? It's the project manager who sees them on the job. How should the line manager assess the performance of their direct reports if they do not see them in action every day? We can continue with simple questions like these and they would all lead to the same conclusion: the traditional work division between line managers and project managers is severely flawed. Accordingly, we reviewed the two roles from scratch. We started by taking a look at the basic Leadership Portrait for a leader-of-others.

The reality is, no matter how you've organized your business, the basic job to be done doesn't go away—the question is who should do what part of the job.

In this specific case, we defined who should do what in relation to the employees. In Table 11.1 we've illustrated a short version of the conclusion we came to. The point is the line manager and project manager play different roles and that an organization needs

Table 11.1. Role Differences Between a Line Leader and a Project Leader.

Work to Be Done	Line Leader	Project Leader
Set direction	Define function standards and instill company values.	Define the business objectives and prioritize the work.
Empower	Free up people to work exclusively on the projects.	Delegate work and enable employees to complete their work.
Development	Define the long-term development plan and the short-term development goals. Provide function learning opportunities and coaching.	Coach and provide feedback to employees while on their projects. Link coaching and feedback to the development plan.
Performance assessment	Collect performance input from the project manager. Conduct formal performance review conversations.	Provide the employees with feedback on how they perform. Create structured input to the line manager on the performance of employees.
Selecting	Select people externally and assign them to projects. Secure diversity in the workforce.	Provide input to the line manager on what type of people and capabilities are needed—both short and long term.
Build the team	Create team feeling among direct reports.	Build a high-performing project team and drive engagement.

both roles to be played. Both managers need to understand the differences, and so do the employees. The key to success is the interaction between the line manager and the project manager, for which you need to establish a simple process.

The outcome of the case included the following. The company defined separate Leadership Portraits for the line manager and the project manager. Future project managers wouldn't just attend project manager certification training; they would also attend leadership transition training alongside the line managers. That the line managers and project managers were trained on the same programs was one of the key elements of getting the information exchange process between them to work.

One aspect of this case applies to the Leadership Pipeline model as a whole: when you map the leadership roles within an organization, don't just look at what job is being done by the leaders. Ask, "What is the job that *should* be done by the leader?" Although you may want to start out attending to the situation as it is, ultimately the real value creation is in defining what *should* be.

Scaled Agile Organizations Leader

Since 2010 or so, a number of new leadership roles have emerged in the slipstream of agile organizational principles. Examples of leadership roles include tribe lead, chapter lead, squad lead, product lead (owner), people lead, and others. Five to 10 years ago we experienced that, when parts of the organization "went agile" (typically the IT function, later on also other functions), the agile portion turned its back on the Leadership Pipeline model even though 90% of the organization was subscribed to it. This was based on the misconception that the Leadership Pipeline model equals only the framework illustrated in Chapter 1. Today, it is appreciated that people in the different agile leadership roles benefit from having a defined Leadership Portrait—and that, to be successful in their roles, they must make a transition in work values, time application, and skills.

In our work with agile organizations, we've found variations in role types and role definitions—depending on the size and maturity of the organization and depending on which consultancy company supported the organization in implementing the agile structure. (See Figure 11.1.) To explain how the Leadership Pipeline model also helps organizations with an agile setup, we will elaborate on three of the roles to illustrate how the Leadership Pipeline model has been used. Though this setup may not be exactly how your organization is designed, it is representative of most agile setups we've been exposed to.

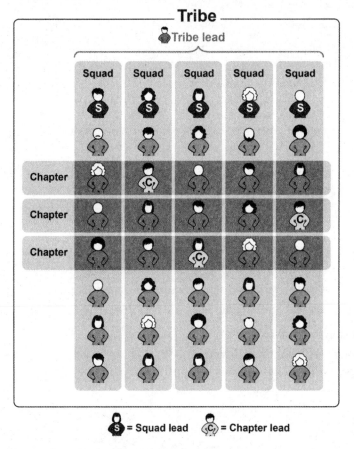

Figure 11.1. Example of an Agile Structure.
Source: Copyright Leadership Pipeline Institute.

Squad Lead

The squad lead is responsible for the squad delivering on time and at the right quality. For matters of product delivery, they report to the tribe leads.

They plan the execution of work and build a strong team, but they don't take the traditional leader-of-others role. The key to their success is building a self-leading team; the squad lead nurtures the team to allocate their time among team members, plan their own work, step in for colleagues, and problem-solve as a team. Though squad leads lead the squad, they avoid micromanaging and exercise little control.

And though squad leads are expected to provide coaching, feedback, and inspiration, they are not in charge of the squad members' development or performance process per se. That role falls to the chapter leads, who reach out to get input on the performance and development needs of their chapter members.

Chapter Lead

The chapter lead serves the leader-of-others role for squad members. They are responsible for ensuring that the members selected for a squad have the tools and skills needed to complete a particular deliverable. They do this by developing the existing staff members and strategically sourcing talent outside the organization— essentially building the chapter for the future. This includes developing some members to take on squad lead roles.

In assessing performance and developing the squad leads and squad members, the chapter leads work closely with the tribe leads and depend on feedback from the tribe leads. Likewise, chapter leads collect performance input from squad leads and other relevant stakeholders across the tribe. They rely on this input when providing performance feedback to chapter members, when assigning chapter members to the squads, and when developing the required capabilities for the future.

The chapter lead needs to (1) value developing people and seeing people grow, (2) view themselves as leaders, and (3) value the success of the entire value chain as they deliver resources across squads.

From a time application perspective, the chapter lead role is usually not a pure leadership role. The chapter lead is also part of a squad and contributes alongside other squad members.

In Figure 11.2 we have illustrated one client example on how the leadership job to be done can be captured for a chapter lead.

Tribe Lead

A tribe is a collection of squads with interconnected missions. The role of the tribe lead is to create value within the tribe for the end customer. They create the overall plan for what needs to be

The Work	Required Activities
Develop chapter members	• Set specific development objectives for chapter members. • Provide constructive and fact-based feedback. • Continuously include coaching as part of their leadership style.
Follow through on performance of chapter members	• Collect performance input from tribe lead and squad leads. • Make thorough and fact-based assessments of chapter members. • Respond in a timely manner to individual performance challenges and does not let performance challenges escalate.
Select members for the chapter	• Select qualified chapter members who contribute well to overall chapter performance. • Make the tough decisions and proactively replace chapter members who consistently fall short of delivering on their objectives. • Select chapter members who hold potential to develop into other roles too.
Build the chapter	• Create an inclusive environment where knowledge sharing and collaboration is valued. • Secure diversity in the chapter. • Create an open and trusting environment that encourages people to speak up.
Integrate upwards and sideways	• In due course, share anticipated operational obstacles with the tribe lead. • In due course, share anticipated people strategic challenges with the hierarchical manager. • Share best practices on people matters with peer chapter leads.

Figure 11.2. Chapter Lead: The Job to Be Done.
Source: Copyright Leadership Pipeline Institute.

delivered and how it should be delivered. They prioritize across squads, distribute budgets, determine how much to invest in different efforts, and manage the boundaries shared with other tribes.

Tribe leads don't "own" the people working within the tribe. They work through the chapter leads to identify and select the right people for each squad. However, they are responsible for setting and nurturing the overall tribe culture.

The tribe lead role is usually a full-time role. They are not engaged in producing any products.

A successful tribe lead must develop solid business acumen. They manage business objectives and prioritize across the tribe. They need a strategic, cross-functional, profit-and-loss mindset. Because the tribe lead is a pure leadership role, from a work values perspective they need to value creating results through the squads within the tribe and creating success across the value chain.

In Figure 11.3 we've illustrated one client example on how work values, time application, and skills could be defined for the tribe lead role.

When looking across these three roles, note that the overall leadership job to do does not go away even when within an agile organization. The leadership work is simply distributed differently, especially in that it relies much more on self-leading teams.

We have seen companies struggle when they implement the scaled agile framework. They can experience an immediate energy boost from the new organizational setup, but all too often frustration sets in later, especially among chapter leads and tribe leads. This happens when the companies don't provide structured transition training for the key agile leadership roles—leaving them ill prepared, struggling to find time for the leadership work, and, often, struggling to even value the leadership work.

To reiterate: applying the Leadership Pipeline model calls for (1) mapping the leadership roles in scope, (2) defining the job to be done for each role, and (3) defining the required work values, time application, and skills for each role. When properly applied, the model can work in many variations of scaled agile organizations.

Tribe lead

WORK VALUES
- Achieving results through squads
- Success in value chain
- Ambiguity
- Values-based leadership

TIME APPLICATION
- Annual planning
- Resource allocation
- Managing boundaries between squads
- Managing boundaries to peer tribes

SKILLS
- Setting the tribe culture
- Selecting squad leaders and squad members
- Assessing performance of squad/chapter leads
- Foster diversity and inclusion across the tribe
- Business acumen

Figure 11.3. Tribe Lead: Work Values, Time Application, and Skills.
Source: Copyright Leadership Pipeline Institute.

Leader of Contractors

We have worked with a number of companies who depend on a large number of external contractors. Given the current labor market, we also see more traditional companies using contractors as an alternative to employees. In these companies, the traditional organizational charts don't tell the whole story when you map the leadership roles.

Case study

We worked with a traditional insurance company that had about 7,000 employees. They also had a sales force made up of thousands of sales representatives. The sales representatives are not employees; they are independent contractors with sales representative contracts. They are primarily paid by commissions.

This company had mapped their organization in accordance with the Leadership Pipeline model several years earlier. But because they were not comfortable with the results, they asked us to help them make it work. On a closer examination, we discovered that the mapping was based on the organization chart. Accordingly, all employees without direct-report employees were categorized as individual contributors, and their leaders were categorized as leaders-of-others.

This was a significant flaw in their leadership framework. Most of the individual contributors in the sales organization were responsible for 10 to 15 independent sales representatives (contractors). Their title would properly be *district manager* because they covered a certain city or geographical area. They did not have formal leadership responsibility, but their core value creation was to enable the independent sales representatives to be successful. The company argued that there must be an arms'-length relationship between the district manager and the independent contractors so that the independent contractors would not be legally considered "employees." Consequently, they didn't define district managers as leaders.

You might be able to guess what we thought of this detail. We believe that the title is irrelevant. Whether the role is called *district manager* or *leader-of-others*, the job to be done is the same.

This is true even though the district manager role is not a "full" leader-of-others role because there are certain things that the district managers cannot do. For instance, they can't dictate how the independent contractors prioritize their time or how many hours they work. They can't enforce individual development plans or build teams. But there are many parts of the leader-of-others role that they can do within the legal relationship—and must do if they are to be successful as district managers.

Table 11.2 illustrates a condensed version of these district managers' job to be done in managing the independent contractors—including the variations in terms of how they are not completely leaders-of-others.

Again, though there are clearly variations to this role, the work values, time application, and skills of the district managers matched 80% of the leader-of-others role.

The insurance company ended up defining a full Leadership Portrait for the district managers, and thereafter included them in the company's regular leader-of-others transition programs, even though 20% of the program content wasn't relevant to them.

Table 11.2. Case Study District Managers: The Job to Be Done.

The Standard Work of Leading Leaders	The Required Activities of These District Managers
Set direction.	Provide sales targets per product and targets for desired client mix.
Empower.	Not applicable; the contractor operates with full autonomy.
Develop contractors.	Offer informal support to the contractor in getting better at their job without enforcing formal development plans. (It is up to the contractor to complete product training, compliance training, and sales training.)
Follow through on performance.	Provide the same leadership as leading others—just not using the company forms usually used for employees.
Select contractors.	Provide the same leadership of leading others—with the exception of preparing them for other roles.
Build the team.	Not relevant.
Integrate upwards and sideways.	Provide the same leadership as leading others.

An equally important adjustment was made to the leaders to whom district managers reported. Originally, they had been classified as leaders-of-others. But because they were actually leaders-of-leaders, their success criteria needed to include helping the district managers drive results through the independent sales representatives. This detail exemplifies how the Leadership Pipeline model represents a systemic approach to developing all leaders and holding all leaders accountable. If you get one layer wrong, then it affects other layers, too.

We included this case to illustrate the importance of looking beyond the formal organization chart when mapping leadership roles. The focus must be on how the different roles create unique value.

Section Leader

When we work with very large organizations, we often see a variation of the leader-of-leaders role that we call the *section leader* role. Unfortunately, this role is often not recognized as being a distinct role—which can make companies' business execution and succession planning very challenging.

To illustrate this role we'll describe one of the companies we've worked with. The company has about 65,000 employees. They've organized themselves as one business. They have one business leader and eight function leaders. The product development function has about 24,000 employees, who are divided into six layers—as illustrated in Table 11.3.

The two lower levels of employees—frontline employees and agile leaders—are organized based on the scaled agile framework principles for enterprises. Above them are about 600 leaders-of-leaders. The interesting level is the next level, the section leader level.

Initially, the company thought they had two levels of leaders-of-leaders—including the section leaders—and they treated these

Table 11.3. The Six Layers of One Company's Product Development Employees.

Position	Number of Employees
Product head(s)	1
Product function leaders	12
Section leaders	100
Leaders-of-leaders	600
Agile leaders	3,000
Frontline employees	20,000

two levels the same way for leadership development and leadership performance assessment. But what they realized during the people review and succession planning processes was that most of the lower-level leaders-of-leaders would not be considered candidates for the higher-level leaders-of-leaders roles.

This was because the job to be done and the required work values, time application, and skills are different between the two roles. Accordingly, we cannot expect everyone to be able to perform equally in both roles.

We recommended that the company make a clear distinction between the roles and name the upper-level role *section leader*. To this they replied, "But we don't want all these leadership layers; that's why we name them the same." We then offered the response that always applies in these situations: "It is not the Leadership Pipeline model that creates your leadership layers—they are already there. The Leadership Pipeline model just helps you and your leaders make sense of the already existing leadership layers."

Let's examine some of the typical differences between the leader-of-leaders and section leader roles.

The leaders-of-leaders in this case lead between 30 and 50 people, whereas the section leaders lead between 200 and 300 people. Accordingly, the operations leader is not involved in any frontline work; it's exclusively a leadership role. The key to success is the ability to lead through multiple leadership layers and design an effective organization structure.

Most people find this role challenging. They are two layers away from the business leader and three layers away from the frontline employees. Their direct reports—the leaders-of-leaders—often consider them in their way for getting decisions from the function leadership team, and their direct managers (the product function leaders) often consider them in the way of getting information about the frontline activities. Many refer to the layer of section leaders as the layer of concrete—nothing gets past it in either direction. But that view doesn't change the fact that, in large organizations, this role is key to managing resources and efficiency across the function. Also, it's a key steppingstone for leaders aspiring to the function leader role. In fact, one of the challenges to this role is when section leaders *only* see holding the role as a steppingstone—rather than valuing the role as it is.

To avoid these challenges, organizations need to both clearly define this role and help the leaders developing into this role.

Section leaders need to focus on the following:

- Allocating resources

- Managing boundaries with peer organization units

- Selecting and developing leaders-of-leaders

- Designing the organization

- Planning long-term talent

- Providing input to the function strategy

The two primary resources they manage are money and people. They need to continuously prioritize and reprioritize these resources across the teams reporting to them. Because these are usually tough decisions, making good friends can be challenging. As for time allocation, they often find they need to spend more than half their time away from their own organization, mostly with peers and in relation to external sourcing. Another 25% of their time goes to addressing employees' needs. In organizations of this size, there are always vacancies that the section leader must fill. Also, it's critical that they dedicate time for long-term planning: on what type of capabilities are needed, where will people be sourced (geographically), how to organize people, and how to identify talent.

About 80% of the leaders-of-others that we meet in our leadership transition programs claim that (1) they are not explicitly held accountable for leadership performance and (2) most of their direct managers don't develop them as leaders. This is a critical issue for organizations. The root cause of this problem is usually one (and sometimes all) of the following three considerations:

- The section leader selects the wrong leaders-of-leaders.

- The section leader doesn't hold the leaders-of-leaders accountable for developing leadership talent.

- The section leader does not develop the leaders-of-leaders reporting to them.

If we don't internalize this concept, any organization will suffer from a shortage in leadership talent. Given the size of the organization led by section leaders, they clearly have great opportunity to develop employees. Equally important, they can sit down with peers and plan cross-organizational career moves for talented people. This latter detail requires maturity from the section leaders because it involves promoting their own best talent to other parts of the company.

Group Leader

The traditional group leader role as described in previous editions of this book seems to be disappearing as organizations flatten and fewer companies are run as conglomerates. However, we see the role emerging in a lighter version that makes sense for large integrated organizations.

Challenges of the Role

The first challenge of the group leader role is often its very definition. A group leader is characterized by having a portfolio (whether three, five, or more) of *independent* businesses reporting to them—independent in the sense that one business could be spun off with minimal impact on the other businesses. Each business has its own business leader with full business leader responsibility as described in Chapter 6.

A common problem we've seen is companies in which one of the business leaders runs their business and has other businesses reporting to them in addition, making them also a de facto group manager.

Business leaders usually love their jobs—running one's own business can be enormously rewarding—but shifting roles to group executive calls for significant change. Sometimes they lack a staff to tend to this portion of their responsibilities and must borrow staff members from business unit or the corporation itself. Also, the skills required at this level are more subtle and indirect. Group executives must engage in the occasionally frustrating work of allocating limited corporate resources among competing businesses, developing business leaders without stepping on their toes, and developing an appropriate portfolio strategy that not only creates horizontal synergy among various business units but also identifies new businesses, as appropriate. Group leaders must also assess business leaders, their teams, and their cultures as though they were the sole owners of those business units, demanding performance and externally driven goals. In other words, they have to shift from the most-fun leadership position to the least fun. Some group executives tell us they slog their way through this role only because they view it as a steppingstone to a CEO position.

Benefits of the Role

However, organizations that truly understand the potential of this role require a group strategy to be developed, usually global in scope, that encompasses issues such as unserved markets, unaddressed customer segments, and likely increases in required capacity. Many of these savvy companies also make group executives responsible for driving critical initiatives down through the organization, and they test how well these executives build external relationships for the whole enterprise by assigning them government, industry, or key customer responsibilities. When group executive responsibilities are broadened in this manner, the role expands to include more than just supervision of business leaders; it involves being tested for CEO potential by doing some CEO work. Done correctly, the role provides experience leading multiple (and often diverse) business units.

But, even apart from that, this group executive role is also a pivotal level for any organization. Leadership pipelines often become clogged because group executives either aren't prepared for this leadership transition or aren't supported while holding the role, or both. As a result, they can usurp the functions of their business leaders, which brings their business leaders to usurp the role of their functional managers, and so on down the line. In effect, they start a chain reaction in which everyone pushes their direct reports down one leadership level.

What Success in the Role Looks Like

There are some parallels here with the leadership transition to a first-time manager. In both cases, people have to give up work they really enjoyed doing and that defined their previous success. They must relinquish their hands-on responsibilities for more ephemeral and less immediately satisfying tasks. In some instances, this can even mean tearing down something they've built; for example, they may have to reduce resources to or even shut down a business they had developed to accommodate changing market conditions or overall portfolio strategy objectives.

It is absolutely essential that group executives are able to *succeed indirectly* by valuing the success of their business and that of the business leaders who run those businesses. Cognitively, this may be a foreign concept to highly ambitious, results-oriented people who become group leaders. As much as they've learned to delegate and coach at earlier leadership levels, this would be the first time they've needed to cede to others just about all direct involvement in running an entity. This would also be the first time they must spend significant time thinking about a collection of businesses as well as their relationship to the larger corporation. Judging the strategic skills of business managers and using their power and influence to approve projects are just two requirements they would not have had at earlier leadership levels. As one discontented group executive shared with us, "I just can't do anything. Hands-on business is what I get a kick out of and it's why my last job was great. Now the fun is gone."

Success, therefore, comes through a different path and calls for a particular mindset:

- Successful group managers make good decisions that differentiate between businesses on the basis of likely results (rather than personal preference).

- Successful group managers work with their direct reports to grow them as business leaders.

- Successful group managers are able to prioritize a portfolio of strategies over individual strategies.

In other words, the goal is no longer to grow one's own business but to create the right mix of investment in a number of businesses.

This means weighing the pros and cons of growing one business through investment versus harvesting another business for cash that could generate growth capital for other businesses. It may also mean looking at different countries and customer groups in terms of growth prospects and making investment decisions accordingly. Determining how Wall Street might assess a move is also crucial here. As you can guess, this is a much more complex, ambiguous process than investing resources in just one business. It requires the ability to critique strategy—not just develop it.

This role is quite difficult for many group managers because it's primarily a nurturing, hands-off role. The biggest mistake group managers can make is to assume some or all of a business leader's responsibilities or dictate a strategy for a business rather than letting the business manager learn on their own. Again, the problem relates to what group leaders value. Most come into the job valuing a more involved, interactive relationship with direct reports—only to need to step back and be more Socratic in their supervisory style.

Many group leaders reflexively focus on individual strategies for individual businesses, often because in the past they valued the performance of one business. This perspective can often be an obstacle for the portfolio strategy necessary at this level. What's required is multidimensional thinking, integrating a variety of business needs and issues into a holistic plan. Again, this is a much more indirect way of viewing strategic planning than most managers are used to.

On a concluding note, we'd like to emphasize that the Leadership Pipeline model is a set of leadership first principles. Accordingly, they can be used in any organizational structure to map the job to be done for a given leadership role and to determine what the required work values, time application, and skills are. The more simple an organization structure you have, the easier it is. But the more complex an organization structure you have, the more important it becomes.

We said at the beginning of this chapter that the scenarios shared here are just some of those that companies have experienced in adapting the Leadership Pipeline concepts for new structures. If you needed to translate the principles into yet another type of role or structure, we'd love to hear from you. Let us know what you did. If it's working well for you, we'd like to share your process with others. If it's not working well for you, we'd like to help you fix it. We know we can because every leadership role can be accounted for with the Leadership Pipeline model.

The Authors

R am Charan is a best-selling author, teacher, and world-renowned advisor to CEOs and other business leaders of some of the world's best-known companies, including Toyota, Bank of America, Aditya Birla Group, Novartis, Fast Retailing (Uniqlo), and Humana.

The author of close to 40 books, four of which were best-sellers, he is known for providing real-world solutions—the kind of advice you can use Monday morning. His book *Execution*, lauded for its practicality, spent more than 150 weeks on the *New York Times* best-seller list.

Ram has an MBA with high distinction and a doctorate degree from Harvard Business School, where he was a Baker Scholar and faculty member.

Steve Drotter is chairman of The Leadership Pipeline Institute, which is dedicated to advancing the knowledge and practices for developing leaders for current and future positions. He has lead the human resource function in two major companies. He founded Drotter Human Resources in 1985.

For almost 50 years Steve has worked with succession planning and leadership development both as the internal leader of the work and as an executive consultant to over 100 companies on five continents in 37 countries. He has completed 30 CEO succession plans and installed or revised succession planning in 40 companies. As part of this work he has completed 1,500 in-depth executive assessments of candidates for CEO, COO, CFO, CHRO, and business general manager. These interviews provide the source material for this book.

Steve is the author of *The Performance Pipeline* and lead author of *The Leadership Pipeline, The Leadership Pipeline Revised and Updated, The Succession Pipeline* and *Pipeline to the Future: Succession and Performance Planning for Small Business.*

Steve has a degree in economics from Amherst College and is a graduate of GE's Human Resource Program.

Before becoming CEO of The Leadership Pipeline Institute, Kent Jonasen was deputy head of Group Human Resources at A.P. Moller–Maersk from 2003 up to 2008, responsible for talent management, leadership development, executive development, and executive compensation. Previous to his deputy position, Kent was regional HR manager for the Europe Region from 2000 to 2003.

At A.P. Moller–Maersk Kent led the implementation of a companywide integrated leadership development initiative based on the Leadership Pipeline concept to affect more than 10,000 leaders in more than 100 countries. The impact of the project was significantly improved scores on "my manager" questions in the engagement survey, increased reliability in succession planning, and a 90% hit ratio on talents in the executive talent pool.

Since founding The Leadership Pipeline Institute Kent has led the implementation of the Leadership Pipeline and Specialist Pipeline concept with regard to development, selection, and assessment in more than 50 different large international organizations.

Kent is the author of the book *Specialist Pipeline: How to Win the War for Specialist Talent*, published in 2023.

Before joining human resources at A.P. Moller–Maersk in 1996 Kent was employed in the financial industry. He worked in retail banking for two years and in the capital market business for three years.

Index